SOCIOECONOMIC
STRATIFICATION

SOCIOECONOMIC
STRATIFICATION

A CASE STUDY ON SUSTAINABLE GROWTH IN A DECLINING POPULATION

Sunday Christopher Enubuzor, Ph.D

Copyright © 2012 by Sunday Christopher Enubuzor, Ph.D.

Library of Congress Control Number: 2012904521
ISBN: Softcover   978-1-4691-8139-4
          Ebook   978-1-4691-8140-0

All rights reserved. No part of this book may be reproduced or transmitted in any form or by any means, electronic or mechanical, including photocopying, recording, or by any information storage and retrieval system, without permission in writing from the copyright owner.

This book was printed in the United States of America.

To order additional copies of this book, contact:
Xlibris Corporation
1-888-795-4274
www.Xlibris.com
Orders@Xlibris.com

TABLE OF CONTENTS

Dedication 11
Acknowledgments 13

Chapter 1 15

    Introduction 15
    The Socioeconomic Changes in US Rural Counties 17
    Qualitative and Quantitative Scope of Data Collection 21
    Theoretical Assertions on Population and
    Economic Growth 22
    Summary 25

Chapter 2 26

    Socio and Economic Circles 26
    The Contemporary Theorists Influences on
    Socioeconomic Circle 29
    Lucas's Influence on Modern Economic Development 35
    Dimension of Population and Economic Formation 39
    Regional and Equity Theoretical Model 42
    Summary 44

Chapter 3 45

    Methodological Approach on Population and
    Economic Growth 45
    Quantitative Design Initiatives 45
    Qualitative Design Initiatives 46
    Case Study Research Initiatives 47
    Mixed-Methods Research Initiatives 48
    Research Setting and Sample Implications 49

Instrumentation and Material Implications................................49
Reliability and Validity Implications...50
Pilot Study Implications 52
Research Questions and Hypotheses Implications 54
The Data Collection Implications 54
The Data Analysis Implications 56
Participants' Sensitivity Initiatives..59
Summary 59

Chapter 4 60

Research Instrumentation Initiatives..60
Research Documentations...61
Sampling Selection Initiatives 62
Collection and Conversion of Data..63
Survey Participants' Demographic Classifications 64
Survey Design Initiatives 65
Descriptive Analysis of the Demographic Data...........................66
Descriptive Analysis of the Independent Variables 67
Descriptive Analysis of the Dependent Variables.......................67
The Survey Results Initiatives 68
The Interview Results Initiatives 69
The Results of the Statistical Data Analysis................................70
The Qualitative Coding Results 72
The Quantitative Results...75
Summary 77

Chapter 5 78

Interpretation of Findings Based on Research Questions..........78

    Research Question 1 78
    Research Questions 2 and 3 80
    Research Question 4 83

Construction of Population Stabilization
and Economic Growth Model..84
Social Change Implications 87

Recommendations for Sustainable Growth
In A Declining Population..89
The Researcher's Personal Reflections 90
Summary 90

Glossary..91
References 95
Appendix A 101
Profile 104

LIST OF TABLES

Table 1. Relationship Between Research Questions
and Survey-Interview Questions 50

Table 2. Pierce County Population 61

Table 3. Pierce County School Enrollment 61

Table 4. Pierce County Revenues, Expenditures,
Fund Balances 1997-2007 62

Table 5. Survey Sample Response Rate 66

Table 6. ANOVA: Economic Growth and
Population Decline 71

LIST OF FIGURES

Figure 1.   Economic growth stem-leaf plot 75

Figure 2.   Simple linear regression slope 76

DEDICATION

I dedicate this book to my beloved wife, Dr. Harriet L. Enubuzor, MD. My children: Chukwuma, Ekeze, Emeka, Christine, and Catherine. Grandchildren: Nikita and DeShawn. They are the love of my life.

ACKNOWLEDGMENTS

I am grateful to my beloved wife, Dr. Harriet L. Enubuzor, MD., and children, Chukwuma, Ekeze, Emeka, Christine, and Catherine Enubuzor. They have given me the optimum support and encouragement throughout the process of writing this book and I am so grateful for them. They are always the love of my life.

CHAPTER 1

Introduction

The relationship between population and economic growth has been insufficiently studied. This research gap is especially noticeable with regards to counties in most developed countries experiencing declining population. Little information is available to help counties stabilize their populations to encourage long-term economic growth. Bucci and Torre (2009) argued that despite the theoretical and empirical researches that were performed by most economists and demographers, they have not produced a shared view on the correlation between population change and economic growth. Tournemaine (2007) supported Bucci and Torre's (2009) assertions and suggested that economic growth depends positively on technological progress and human capital investment.

The economic well-being of U.S. counties is influenced, in part, by government policies. Lee, Harvey, and Neustrom (2002) documented the effects of government incentives to encourage high-tech industries to set up business in particular counties. Dasgupta (2007) stated that innovation in science and technology are necessary for economic growth and that innovation requires a skilled labor force in manufacturing industries and financial institutions. Duesterberg (2007) and Mollick (2006) proposed that skilled labor growth plus productivity contributes to long-term economic growth. Mollick posed several questions that are pertinent for county administrators: What strategies will help stabilize population? What impact will population decline have on long-term economic growth and on the elderly population?

Sound fiscal policies on local growth economy should be sustainable over the long term because all savings are volunteered and savings and investments have to be at equilibrium at all times to retain steady economic growth. Zhang (2010) supported the notion that the productivity parameter of a region as a result of technological advancement will create a propensity to consume goods which will invariably increase county tax rates revenues. Thus, tax parameter serve as an externality for revenue accumulation for the county. Mitchell and Mosler (2006) proposed that policy makers should stimulate growth by promoting education. They argued that long-term economic growth cannot be discussed without considering population stabilization, a claim echoed by Chen (2006). Mollick (2006) also found that the relationship between economic growth and population in some Texas counties in the 1990s resulted from a connection between economic growth and technologically advanced clusters of industries.

It is observed that economic changes are influenced by labor productivity, technology, resource availability, and market availability. Konstantinos (2006) studied the relationship between income and population in urban areas and concluded that population growth in urban areas resulted from migration prompted by people's search for higher paying jobs in the professional, financial, and business service industries. Konstantinos indicated that rural population stability during the 1970s was due to temporary economic factors, such as, homesteaders including increasing commodity prices and agricultural equipment.

With regards to the present demographical socioeconomic situations in most local counties in the United States, as reported by observers, it is apparent that the future of local counties socioeconomic dynamics is not any different on the kind of demographic inputs in population declination that may hamper long-term sustainable growth. According to Eberstadt (2010), today's affluent Western and Japanese economies are faced with a demographic challenge of stagnant and aging populations that are combined with mounting health and pension claims on a shrinking pool of prospective workers. He also indicated these demographic constraints can be substantially offset only if local authorities undertake profound and far-reaching changes in working arrangements, business practices to fuel future growth, and government policies on emigration and lifestyles. Atoh

(2006) argued that the principal socioeconomic issue of today is how a smaller population of workers will support a growing elderly population. In Japan, which is aging rapidly, the percentage of the population of those 65 and older was predicted to increase from 20.9% (1995) to 59.1% (2009). This shift means that industrialized regions will face labor shortages and increasing demands for social services, developments that will hamper economic growth and standard of living. This trend is exacerbated by the fact that fertility rates in most industrialized nations have stayed below replacement levels since the 1970s, which refutes the assumption of demographic transition theory that death rate and birth rates will eventually balance and the population will stabilize (Atoh, 2006).

The Socioeconomic Changes in US Rural Counties

In the early 18th century, the Industrial Revolution affected the organization of farm production and the rural population. In the 20th century, there was a shift from small, individual farms to larger, more intensive, and more mechanized agrarian operations (cite). This change has been cited as contributing to increased environmental degradation, emigration to cities, and the socioeconomic stratification of rural populations (Benz, 2006).

Many rural counties have adopted legislation that protects large farms from corporate ownership. Benz (2006) argued that the piecemeal nature of these laws renders them inadequate and that statewide growth management programs are necessary to address problems associated with farming and non-farming aggregation and population concerns. For example, the Homestead Act was originally passed in 1862 and expanded in 1909. This federal legislation spurred settlement of the American frontier and helped rural communities set up venture capital funds and tax credits for local entrepreneurs.

In 2009, the researcher observed that one of the US Northern County's biggest industrial employers, Rugby Manufacturing in Rugby, North Dakota which makes truck canopies, caps, and shells, lay off about half of its workforce due to the effects of a nationwide recession. No precise estimates of the employee retrenchment were disclosed. Rugby Manufacturer previously had about 250 full—and part-time employees, with an estimated $100 million payroll (Rugby Manufacturing, 2005). The lay-off of skilled workers had a ripple effect on the local economy, leading to job losses in construction, retail, health care, and financial services. Many skilled workers and their families migrated out of the county in search of jobs in urban areas. Finally, additional stress was put on local government tax revenues.

Because of Rugby Manufacturer's large influence on the local economy, it is possible that the loss in jobs across the county could be as high as 250 jobs, when the ripple effect is taken into consideration. This figure includes directly linked industries such as trucking, services, and retail stores that are supported by Rugby Manufacturing employees. In the long run, the loss of Rugby Manufacturer's jobs will have a severe impact on the county's economy because these lost jobs not only represent higher than average wages but also serve as an economic boost for the county. As has been observed, the county government played a sustainable role as users of manufactured products and has provided incentives to the privately owned company to encourage future growth.

Researchers have not adequately addressed the population decline and socioeconomic dilemmas of rural counties. Although many small city administrators are critical of the status quo, they have initiated no well-founded plans to stabilize their declining population for sustainable long-term economic growth. The lack of information about population decline in small counties in developed countries and the resulting socioeconomic impact is a problem that supersedes any other in the global business community. Most small counties in the rural United States are experiencing decline as a result of population and economic strangulation. A lack of attention regarding this increasingly difficult socioeconomic situation contributes unnecessary economic stress to an already diminished population if adequate steps are not taken to find solutions to the growing problem. The author's intent is to explore the contextual challenges and complexities associated with this issue of stabilizing rural populations to promote long-term economic growth in local counties.

The five conditions of a healthy economy are: government, social services and health, training and education, community resources, and the state of the economy. Government's main responsibility is coordinating these components. Communities should always strive for long-term socioeconomic growth. According to Power (as cited in Sertich, 2004), research universities can do much to help rural areas improve their economies. Jischke (as cited in Sertich, 2004) also supported Power's initiative by indicating that the most effective way to develop knowledge-based economies is to partner with research universities.

Coleman (2008) used Europe as a phenomenon to emphasize that a prolonged emigration reduces population size and that emigrants moving away from particular regions (e.g., remote or depressed rural areas) are a familiar pattern in modern societies and one that invariably affects the industrial capacity of the areas emigrants leave behind.

The author main objective is to have the potential to contribute knowledge gathering that will be the basis for policy formulation and social change. Qualitative and quantitative data were gathered to contribute to a new and effective population stabilization and economic growth model that, if used properly, can be applicable for rural counties. The model emphasizes the importance of education, innovation, and human capital as the factors that will promote population stability and long-term economic growth in rural counties. Researchers have documented that the emigration of skilled labor from rural areas to urban centers has serious economic consequences (Chen, 2006). To stem that movement, government can offer incentives to desirable businesses, often in the form of tax advantages and thus, retaining and developing skilled labor is necessary for long-term economic growth. Despite what is known about the consequences of population decline, most government leaders in rural areas lack concrete strategies for reversing it. The model focuses on such socioeconomic variables such as population, economic development, employment, education, and elderly concerns and needs. If the model proves useful, it would provided an approach that encourages population stabilization and facilitates long-term economic growth, while also, serves as an incentive for additional research.

Malthus (1779) predicted that population, if allowed to grow geometrically, will eventually outstrip a food supply that grows arithmetically. Malthus further postulated that because economic growth results in population growth, even if aggregate income increases, per capita income will remain constant or even decline. Smith (1776) asserted that improving income and increasing capital leads to increased wealth. Smith classified manufacturing and agriculture as central to continuous economic growth. Lucas (1988) formulated an endogenous growth theory that offers a mathematical explanation of technological advancement. The model has led to a new understanding of human capital. Endogenous growth theorists, such as: Barro and Romer (1990); Yakita (2006) assume that governmental policies affect long-term economic growth. They asserted that growth does not become apparent as capital accumulates, but the rate of growth depends on the type of investment. Yakita (2006) argued that if the money supply grows fast enough to create a desirable inflation rate, increased longevity will increase people's net savings and shift their portfolios towards nonmonetary assets, which will eventually cause growth. Endogenous growth theorists agreed on principle on the importance of education and technological change as a proponent to economic development.

Lucas (1988) examined the accumulation of human capital, arguing that to achieve exogenous growth without considering other externalities requires that the accumulation of human capital does not diminish. Lucas assumed that knowledge accumulation is linear; however, Lucas's theory on the relationship between education and growth holds that investment in human capital will affect the rate of growth in consumption. For Lucas, economic growth increases in proportion to increases in human capital. Thus, growth depends on accumulating of human capital, which potentially accounts for limitless economic expansion. A fundamental assumption of endogenous growth theorists is that economic growth is facilitated by government policies. Mencken, Bader, and Polson (2006) argued for the importance of civic involvement by policy makers. Lyson and Tolbert (2003) asserted that competitive-based perspectives in civil engagement boost economic growth.

A local county in North Dakota was used to substantially analyze the sustainability of growth in a declining population. This analysis was based on dependent (Y) and independent (X) variables. The dependent variables were employment, education, human capital, technology, innovation, and economic growth. The independent variables were emigration, mortality rate, fertility rate, elderly needs, and population decline. These variables were used to assess the correlation between population decline and long-term economic growth. The objective was to determine how these variables affect the future progress of the county. The variables were analyzed by quantitative and qualitative methods, including a survey, interviews, and documents. Statistical analysis involved the use of a regression model to determine the linear relationships between variables Y and X. A simple linear regression analysis was also used to validate or invalidate the relationships between variables. A *t* test was used to examine a potential linear relationship between the dependent and the independent variables. This possibility was considered and accounted for by considering how the socioeconomic variables affected each other.

Qualitative and Quantitative Scope of Data Collection

The quantitative portion of this study is represented by numerical data, some of which were derived from county census reports. Other quantitative data were collected through a survey. The qualitative component of the study consisted of individual interviews. A self designed population and economic growth survey (PEGS) instrument was used in this study. (See Appendix A for details). The instrument was also used as the basis for individual interviews. Interviewees were asked to describe their assessment of socioeconomic conditions in their community. They were asked about the economic future of the county retirees, about the advisability of creating 2-year colleges in small demographic counties as supporting tool for businesses, and about what county policy makers can do to reduce the emigration of skilled labor. The time span of archival data collected for the study was limited. Data collection was also constrained by the availability of additional information specific to the county. It is possible that more comprehensive demographic data would have led to refined analysis and more inclusive results. More specific information might have enabled a more comprehensive model of economic development prospects for the county.

The emerging presentation of this research was to demonstrate understanding of the study. The presentation main objectives were to examine and evaluate the effect of emigration, fertility and mortality rate, elderly population standard of living, technology, education, economic growth in the county, and the ability of the local county authority to perform, monitor, and manage a declining population to a sustainable long-term economic growth. The presentation analyzes data from both quantitative and qualitative designs using a mixed-method case study to demonstrate holistically the characteristics of the results from the research.

It is the author's vision to contribute to positive social change by developing strategies to reverse the county's population decline and exodus of skilled labor. Other counties with similar demographics will also benefit from the results of this study. This study can contribute to rural and small-town population stability, long-term economic growth, and improved living standards.

Theoretical Assertions on Population and Economic Growth

Malthus's (1779) population theory and Smith's (1776) theories on economic growth, along with Lucas's (1988) endogenous growth theory, are important to the thinking of most social and economic scientists' approach to population and economic growth. These theorists are not the only ones to have addressed these principles, but the paradigm they represent is central to the assumptions that guided this study. One branch of socioeconomic theory focuses on the correlation between population and economic growth. The purpose of the study was to understand how population dynamics affect economic growth by considering such phenomena as intergenerational solidarity, market institutions, and education.

Gruescu (2007) attempted to integrate population dynamics and economic growth theories. She selected several growth models to analyze how they could be applied to population stability. Gruescu's rationale for her study was the paucity of research on aging populations and the dearth of growth models with an unlimited planning horizon. Prettner and Prskawetz (2010) supported Gruescu's (2007) assertion and indicated that in exogenous growth models the population size, structure of the workforce, and the capital intensity of the workers are linked to economic growth. They also stated that changes in the decomposition of the workforce and an increase in population size will affect aggregate productivity that can boost capital in the population. Bloom and Sousa-Poza (2010) asserted that declining population on an aging population will affect economic growth and lower standard of living. They argued that the effect of population declining in size can be an impediment to economic growth and capital dilution in the population.

Prettner and Prskawetz (2010) postulated that demographic change in models of endogenous economic growth ensures that as technology gets more and more complex, the importance of human capital in final goods production increases. Thus, affect household consumption behavioral pattern, whereby, choices are made between consumption and investment. They asserted that the latter is divided into human capital investments, whose return are higher future wages, invested into new ideas, for a possible return on invested capital. According to Strulik (2005), this model is built with horizontal and vertical innovation that implements endogenous educational decisions and also leads to laws of motion for the technological level and the average quality of labor.

Zhang (2007) argued that the economic geography of a regional economy can have the dynamism anticipated by the work of Solow (1956), which focuses on general equilibrium framework with perfect competition, differences in amenity, technology prone to return to scale, and factors that influences endowments and productivity as against monopolistic competition and scale economics. Baldwin and Martin (2004) also confirmed Solow's work by asserting that capital accumulation can also be determined as a basis of growth theory. Zhang supported their notion and pointed out that the reason capital accumulation and distribution are not adopted as the economic principles of small open economic is perhaps due to analytical tendencies associated with capital accumulation.

Lucas et al. (1988) noted that endogenous growth theory assumes a constant return to capital and that the rate of growth depends on the type of investment. Yakita (2006) argued that if the money supply's growth rate is sufficiently high to create a satisfactory inflation rate, increased longevity will increase total savings and shift investors' portfolios towards nonmonetary assets, which would eventually cause growth. These theories suggest that contributions to a local economy from its elderly residents, in the form of savings and investments, are potentially of great significance.

According to Mencken, Bader, and Polson (2006), another important component of socioeconomic stability and growth is civic engagement by policy makers. Lyson and Tolbert (2003) asserted that with net sales from traditional markets, competitive-based policies informed by civil engagement boost economic growth. Lobao and Hooks (2003) noted that another factor for growth is political elites who exercise disproportionate influence on such things as defense contracts, military bases, and government infrastructure. These notions are important for county authorities to consider in formulating strategic development plans.

According to Mollick (2006), technological expansion, skilled labor migration, and education can influence regional and local economic growth. He noted that economic growth is tied to a high concentration of economic activities. Mollick postulated that investment and income from wages responds proportionately to employment, and that a favorable relationship between the two helps stabilize population and increase economic growth.

Prettner and Prskawetz (2010) argued that while the population size does not matter for the steady economic growth, the effects of population growth on the economy remains ambiguous. However, they asserted that policymakers can influence economic growth, namely through R&D subsidies, which may ensure increases in efficiency of education as well as more competition in the marketplace that would be able to spur economic development in a long-run. Prettner (2009) further argued that population aging can have positive impacts on economic growth if it triggers additional savings or investments into R&D. Population aging can also have negative impacts if pension schemes are designed such that the size of the workforce decreases relative to the amount of retirees.

Zhuang and St. Juliana (2010) argued that economic growth is not measured only by a given population unit's per capita GDP but also reflects its residents' general welfare. They also emphasized that sustainable economic growth is essential for a county's, states, or country's long-term development and stability, and they urged policy makers to exploit those variables that affect economic growth. They cited Solow's model of capital accumulation and population growth as emphasizing the important variables related to economic growth. They also noted that Lucas et al. (1988) postulated that technology progress and human capital are related to labor effectiveness and hence to economic growth. Zhuang and St. Juliana observed that other theorists have examined the impact of education and research and development on economic growth through the channel of improving labor effectiveness. Zhuang and St. Juliana cited completion rate, the proportion of R&D expenditures in GDP, and the percentage of exports and imports in GDP as essential variables that affect sustainable economic growth.

The current study is indebted to the insights of the socioeconomic theorists. One discipline associated with socioeconomic analysis is sociology, which considers human relationships and their functionality. The sociological perspective considers social and environmental influences on human behavior in other to critically assess the facts associated with a particular community of people. Another factor associated with socioeconomic analysis is technology, which Mollick (2006) defined as the mechanical knowledge and processes community of people use to promote economic growth.

Summary

More specifically, the aim of the Significance of the Study section was to review selected endogenous economic growth models and illustrate their predictions on the correlation between demographic development in population dynamics and economic growth. In particular, I reviewed extensions of those models that explicitly examined theoretically and empirically frameworks that influence the demographic change in models of endogenous economic growth, population aging, technological innovation, education, and fertility and mortality rates.

The rationale and purpose for a mixed-methods case study on a sparsely populated county was emphasized in the discussion. The study was to develop a model for population stabilization and economic growth that can assist officials' similar county catastrophes.

CHAPTER 2

Socio and Economic Circles

As Barro (1993) noted, modern economic theory has been heavily influenced by the theoretical concepts of Smith (1776) and Malthus (1779). White and Anderson (2001) used Smith's notions about supply and demand to emphasize that population distribution influences economic development and create openness and flexibility in promoting business development. White and Anderson also argued for the continuing relevance of Smith's supply and demand model, which is based on the equation $Y = f(L, K, T)$, where Y is output, L is labor, K is capital, and T is land in economic development. Mencken, Bader, and Polson (2006) described three sociological theories used in analyzing local economies: human ecology, political economy, and labor market theory. Smith (1776) division of labor model is constrained by markets condition whereby, when there are labor increases, there is a corresponding increase in output. The extent of the market creates the possibility of further growth. Smith's argument about growth depends on increasing returns to scale. He also argued that improving workers' living standards is another way to increase growth potential, cautioning that the contrary would result in a reduced labor supply. Smith saw distribution of income as an important determinant of how societies grow. He noted that saving partly determined by stock profits, and as capital stock increases, profit declines. Smith argued that it is not a decrease in productivity that affects wages but rather the effect of competition for capital that bids wages up.

Ricardo (1817) predicted that machinery would displace labor and that reabsorbing labor would be difficult because capital is not simultaneously available to accommodate both machinery enhancement and labor force recruitment. He also predicted that those jobs that survived would be subject to downward pressure on wages. To reabsorb the labor force, Ricardo argued, the rate of capital accumulation must be increased. Smith (1776), on the other hand, argued that population multiplies in proportion to the means of subsistence, and that as demand for labor increases, rewards for the laborer must be adequate to ensure that supply equates demand.

Malthus's (1779) *The Principle of Population* was written in reaction to Rousseau and others (including Malthus's father) concerning the perfectibility of society. Malthus also was reacting to Marquis de Condorcet and William Godwin. He regarded idealistic visions of the future skeptically, noting that in every human population there has always been one consigned to poverty. Malthus explained this phenomenon by postulating that growth in a population often predates an expansion of resources.

> In all societies, even those that are most vicious, the tendency to a virtuous attachment is so strong that there is a constant effort towards an increase of population. This constant effort as constantly tends to subject the lower classes of the society to distress and to prevent any great permanent improvement of their condition. (Malthus, 1779, p. 65)

Malthus (1779) noted that throughout history societies have experienced famines, wars, and epidemics, events that mask the problem of outstretched resources. He argued that the power of population transcends the earth's power to provide subsistence and that premature death is the only solution to unrestrained population growth. He proposed that population, if unchecked, increases geometrically (2, 4, 8, 16, etc.), while a food supply grows arithmetically (1, 2, 3, 4, 5, etc.). Some commentators have charged that Malthus did not appreciate humans' ability to increase the food supply, noting that food supply in the past 2 centuries has generally kept up with population. The catastrophe Malthus predicted was averted by advances in technology and by an expanded market economy, which were not accounted for in his early theory.

In Malthus's day, many observers considered high fertility an economic advantage because it increased the labor supply. Malthus, on the other hand, considered fertility from a different perspective.

He managed to persuade most economists that although high fertility could raise gross output, it would likely decrease output per capita. Several notable economists, such as David Ricardo and Alfred Marshall, were persuaded by Malthus's argument. His theory led to the Poor Act of Great Britain and helped promote an 1801 national census in the United Kingdom. The United Nations has acknowledged that discussions about the Earth's optimum population began with Malthus. His ideas continue to have remarkable influence in sociological and economic circles.

Malthus (1779) indicated that as wages increase, there is a corresponding increase in birth rates and a decrease in death rates. He speculated that rising incomes allow people to raise more children, which increase the birth rate, and to afford medicines that would ward off fatal diseases, thus decreasing the death rate. Population growth, then, is tied directly to wage increases and other socio benefits. Population growth in turn increases the labor supply, which depresses wages, and in turn, exerts downward pressure on population growth.

Smith's (1776) economic theory stressed the importance of the savings rate, land growth (e.g., colonization), land fertility, technological development, and mobilization of the population through emigration and migration. In Smith's view, technological progress increases economic growth, as do trade and the division of labor through specialization. Trade is an especially powerful engine of growth because it facilitates further specialization. Malthus (1779), on the other hand, asserted that an unchecked population increase without a corresponding increase in food supply will eventually lower a society's standard of living. He criticized welfare practices of the time, arguing that they fostered dependency rather than productivity and that they contributed to rising food prices and high deficits in society's coffers.

Yogi (2005) postulated Knies's (1873) philosophical views of the economic theory with social and political perspectives worked on value-use theory and had influenced many theorists on issues of production, labor, and wages. Knies stated that "capital is the sum of exploited labor" (p. 314) and that state intervention maybe necessary when workers are exploited for profits. Knies (1873) also argued that "the maximum of wages is given by the usable value" (p. 325); in other words, the standards of wages should be determined by the living cost of a worker or his or her family; otherwise, the contrary may lead to an unhealthy standard of living. Yogi (2005) argued that the higher the intensity of want due to production quality of a good the higher the buyer is willing to pay. On the contrary, Knies (1873) indicated that average intensity of individual demand determines the average market price. Knies also criticized the views of some theorists on cost of production as a determinant of price. He further argued that price can only be affected due to increase or decrease in supply or demand.

The Contemporary Theorists Influences on Socioeconomic Circle

Contemporary economic theorists have offered a variety of explanations for how economies develop and change. Menchen, Bader, and Polson (2006) noted that there is a tendency to explain economic growth in terms of a particular influence, such as well-connected politicians or aggressive labor leaders. Lee, Harvey, and Neustrom (2002) observed that a labor market theory that attempts to account for both social ecology and political economy conceives of growth as a result of local labor market conditions. Local labor and productivity capacity allow for economic growth and rising incomes. Lee et al. described mechanized agriculture as central to economic growth. Romer, Lucas, and Barro (1988) were noted for their mathematical explanation of technological advancement as a tool in projecting long-term economic growth.

Dasgupta (2007) argued that there is no single driving force to economic growth; instead, it results from a combination of manufactured capital, human capital, reproduction, and technological advances. Dasgupta recommended that local units of government emphasize innovation, education, and health care. He asserted that education increases the gross domestic product, reduces fertility and child mortality, and results in an increase in overall capital assets.

Zhuang and St. Juliana (2010) asserted that high capital accumulation enhances capital production, which in turn accelerates economic growth. High production growth adds to the available labor force, which will eventually contribute to economic development. Zhuang and St. Juliana described the completion rate as a proxy of human capital because a highly educated workforce tends to improve productivity and, therefore, economic growth. They noted that R&D expenditures are a stimulant to technological advancement, which accelerates economic growth. They also observed that increased exports and imports are an indicator of a larger trade volume that translates to a positive economic growth.

According to Groth, Koch, and Steger (2010), the standard growth model, a semi-endogenous growth framework, is frequently used to measure long-term per capita and the labor force growth rates. They argued that because the models consistently show exponential growth, and that if the framework is employed to evaluate the prospect of future growth, it is predictable that the growth rate will drop to zero. Such a situation will have profound consequences for both population growth and human capital growth. It should be noted that Lucas et al. (1988) formulated an alternative of the semi-endogenous growth model. Also, Groth et al. posited that theirs was a first-generation growth model that accommodated exponential growth with zero population growth.

Yakita (2006) viewed real capital as stored wealth. He was interested in the economic effects of delayed retirement, what influences the savings rate, how investment choices affect economic growth by way capital accumulation, and the differential effects of investment in real (nonmonetary) versus abstract (monetary) goods. The spillover of capital accumulation to labor productivity affects savings and income. Yakita asserted that if the capital spillover effect is sufficiently strong, a decline in mortality will lower the inflation rate as the growth rate increases. An increase in life expectancy will reflect an increase in economic growth.

According to Zhang (2004), research shows that Social Security tends to prompt per capita growth by reducing fertility and by increasing investments in human capital without a corresponding effect on savings. Economic growth per se does not change Social Security contributions or benefits. Zhang emphasized that his analysis was based on a two-sector growth model. He concluded that an aging population can be a dynamic force that enhances human capital and economic growth.

Lee and Mason (2010) noted that low fertility in many developed countries has led to changes in age structure and population growth. They stated that the first effect of low fertility is to reduce population. As smaller groups of children reach employment age, the working-age population decreases and the average age increases, which raises the per capita income of working population. Lee and Mason argued that shifts in age distribution affect changing support ratios and human and physical capital. They projected that lowered fertility rates and slower growth in population will result in increased capital formation and rising per capita income.

Lee and Mason (2010) charged that decision makers too often make decisions without considering the future. Instead, decisions are based on current standards of living. They noted that greater investment in human capital in effect lowers current consumption by raising future consumption. They also noted that the spending decisions of the present generation of workers will determine how resources are allocated between human capital investment and consumption, and that privileging consumption over time which will significantly affect the elderly standard of living. Laincz and Peretto (2006) carefully asserted that long-run growth must begin with identifying the unit of analysis, the presentation of long-run growth policy implications, and the assumptions of economic of scale effect. They maintained that if proper attention is given to R&D and the aforementioned sources of growth policy, adequate standard of living might be raised. Broda and Weinsten (2006) supported Laincz and Peretta assertions on the total aggregation of the sources of growth policy.

Howitt (2007) and Madsen (2008) asserted that Schumpeterian growth theory is the most consistent and current of the growth theories. However, they posed that there is no indication that the Schumpeterian theory would have worked during the Malthusian era. Galor (2005) studied the post Malthusian and modern growth theories and argued that innovation was the key factor that stimulated growth which was the period population declined.

However, according to Madsen, Ang, and Banerjee (2010) and as noted by Craft and Mills (2009), Rosen (2009) argued that "failure attempts by growth economists to model the transition to modern economic growth should perhaps pay more explicit attention to improvements in capabilities and incentive structures that increased the probability of technological advances" (p. 263).

Madsen, Ang, and Banerjee (2010) supported Howitt (1999 and 2007) and Madsen (2008) assertions that Schumpeterian growth theory shows a strong relationship between growth and innovation and that Schumpeterian growth theory assisted the R & D permanent growth effect as far as productivity growth rate remains constant and positive and as long as the number of researcher are in constant proportion with size of population in the product line. Madsen, Ang, and Banerjee argued that innovation and population growth are economically significant determinant of per capital growth.

Monteiro and Pereira (2006) argued that many growth theorists failed to conclude the sustainability of growth through innovation because there was insufficient human capital available, at that time, to deal with the complexity of innovation. However, Howitt and Mayer-Foulkes (2005); Parente and Prescott (2005) asserted that there are two composition of knowledge: technological knowledge and knowledge with the utilization of technology. Thus, they argued that knowledge is infinite and always available to ascertain any complex innovation.

Lee and Mason (2010) observed that declining fertility results in an aging population and a greater burden of dependency. They argued that the elderly standard of living (consumption per adult) can be maintained at high levels with appropriate tradeoffs and that human capital strongly affects productivity. They suggested that increased and decreased fertility can counteract the greater costs of a growing elderly population.

Japan provides an interesting comparison to U.S. economic trends. Clark, Ogawa, Kondo, and Matsukura (2010) noted that Japan's economic future will be affected by dramatic population declines in an increasing aging population size, resulting in a shrinking labor force. They observed that since rates of labor force participation remain steady, the labor force reflects an older, smaller population, which will affect economic growth. Clark et al. stated that a Japanese government 2008 white paper projected a decrease in the labor force by one third between 2000 and 2050, from 67 million to 42 million, unless employers and the government make strategic policy changes. The report included several recommendations for increasing rates of labor force participation among particular groups.

Birchenall (2007) studied the role of economic changes and mortality rates during demographic transition. He developed a model of health transmission that considered traditional patterns of mortality resulting from infectious diseases. The model was based on the assumption that parents make choices about many surviving children they want and that children's survival is a function of child-care investment and parents' resources. The model also addressed how health capital evolves over the life cycle and how parents' and children's health status are linked. The model predicts that the return on health-related investments in children goes beyond increasing survival rates of children because increased standards of living for children indirectly improve adult health and consequently lower adult mortality. Birchenall argued that because investments in children have at least two consequences for survival, economic changes will bring about long-lasting mortality effects not previously noted by researchers. He asserted that economic changes represent the most important influence on mortality rates in developed countries even though there is a weak connection between mortality and income. Improved economic conditions tend to improve health beyond the short term and also to lower adult mortality.

Bezruchka (2009) supported Birchenall's (2007) assertions that recessions have sometimes contradictory effects on mortality rates in developed countries, noting 20th century recessions were associated with declining mortality. He asserted that mortality is procyclical, that it increases during economic expansion and decreases during contractions. Bezruchka noted that during economic booms the rate of decline has been slower, whereas it has bee greater during so-called busts.

Although Birchenall (2007) focused on the early phases of demographic change, her analysis of changes in mortality suggests that declines in mortality among the elderly, which have occurred in developed countries since 1960, are a result of improved medical technology and resulting improvements in health conditions people born between 1900 and 1950, when public health programs began to flourish. She also argued that although declining mortality affects demographic transitions and economic development, theoretical analyses of declining mortality are less common in the literature than are studies exploring fertility changes. Furthermore, it has been argued that most improvements in public health in developed countries took place first in urban rather than rural areas.

According to Bezruchka (2009), economic growth affects health by enabling people to acquire sufficient food, shelter, and potable water, and to receive basic health care. He noted, however, that economic growth will not necessarily result in better health. For example, studies of developed countries suggest that increased wealth, by most measures, does not always improve human welfare. The United

States, for example, has the world's highest GNP per capita but has a lower life expectancy than most developed countries, along with higher levels of poverty, poor health outcomes, and health disparities. Bezruchka asserted that health in developed countries is not based on wealth or economic growth per se but on how a country's resources are shared. He noted that as U.S. inequality of income has increased, relative improvements in health have declined and greater disparities in health have occurred. He concluded that for an advanced country like United States to experience better health for its population, more egalitarian income distribution is required.

Marder and Bansal (2009) used data on life expectancy and mortality to look at the relationship between health and economic growth from 1920 to 1940. Specifically, they examined the relationship between health indicator fluctuations and economic changes. According to Marder and Bansal, the health of the U.S. population during that time either stayed stable or improved. They found a decrease in mortality for most ages and an increase in life expectancy in all demographic groups. The period under consideration, the Great Depression and its aftermath, was marked by significant economic hardship. During the economic expansion that began at the end of the period Marder and Bansal studied, mortality rates increased. In short, recessionary periods were marked by mortality declines and life expectancy gains. One exception was suicide. The rose during the Depression, but they represented less than 2% of deaths during that period. Marder and Bansal's analysis also confirmed a negative relationship between health and economic expansion, thus confirming the counterintuitive hypothesis that the health of a population is better during recessions than during economic expansions. Bezruchka (2009) confirmed Marder and Bansal's conclusion about the effect that economic downturns have on health by observing that birth weights and infant mortality are improved for children born when unemployment rates are high, in part because mothers are freer to devote themselves to child care. Bezruchka added that this phenomenon was non inconsistent with studies suggesting that much adult health is predicted early in life.

Chen (2006) proposed a model for investigating the influence of economic growth affected by migration. Chen assumed that fertility and education decisions are formed by emigrating adults before migration to urban centers. He used a stochastic model to predict that economic growth will more likely reflect migration in a population that primarily uses private education than those that practices public education system. Chen argued that one of government's responsibilities is to increase the potential for economic growth by imposing restrictions on the migration of skilled workers.

Lucas's Influence on Modern Economic Development

For Lucas (1988), education is the chief engine of economic growth. He saw knowledge residing in people rather than goods. Lucas considered human capital as a complement to technical progress. For Lucas, then, the production sector depends on the educational sector. The production of goods requires both human capital and physical capital, and the latter is increased primarily through education.

Lucas's economic theory can be expressed formulaically as follows:

> h(t) = $h(t)$ @[1 — u(t)]. The effort expended on accumulating human capital, $1-u$ (t), reflects variations in its level: $h(t)$. Lucas assumed that the accumulation knowledge follows a linear path, but it is also possible that the stock of knowledge is subject to threshold effects.

Fay (2009) argued that Lucas (1988) assertion that mathematical analysis has been the key progress in economics and the only outlet of venturing into economic theory are narrow in scope. Romer (1980) supported Fay's remarks and also emphasis that the mathematical modeling can lead to neglect of important economic issues. Romer further argued that increasing mathematical theories on economic theory is not equivalent to increasing economic knowledge. Fay (2009) proposed that the key concepts that underlie the model of macroeconomics, like labor substitution, rational expectations, and pricing are neither proven nor disproved simply because of mathematical modeling that are involved in the process. Fay argued that due to uncertainty regarding fundamental economic issues, the construction of elaborate mathematical calculations before the facts can be misleading and construed as "premature optimization" (p. 196). As a result, Fay posed that decision-making process is a model tool that seems inefficient from a perspective of complete knowledge;

in retrospect, a situation of uncertainty is actually the best model tool available.

Temin (2010) in his recent study made observations of John Maynard Kaynes and Karl Marx. As cited by Temin, Kaynes stated, "Practical men who believe they are quite exempt from any intellectual influence are usually the slaves of some defunct economists" (p. 115). Also, cited by Temin, Marx asserted that "the first time as tragedy, the second as farce" (p. 115). These two quotes are noteworthy in regards to decision-making principles. Temin argued that decision makers had avoided tackling socioeconomic imbalances that may pose dramatic and costly future economic crises.

Trichet (2010) supported Temin (2010) assertions and stated decision makers should be more assertive in their responses. Koo (2008) posed that in an open recovery system decision making has to be swift and divergence. Temin (2010) argued that a good marketing decision such as flexibility in pricing in a competitive market has to be well defined taking into consideration changes in products and labor and other economic mechanisms that will ascertan growth or profitability of the firm. Wessel (2009) indicated that changes in the economic theories over time should be taking into consideration in decision making. He supported Temin's assertions that changes in the sizes of business, products, diminished labor bargaining power, noncompetitive market, outsourcing, and a deluge of economic mechanisms affects profitability.

Temin (2010) posed that since economic forecast cannot be determined for certainty due to changes over time. He asserted that economists sometimes overlooked some of the economic imbalance that have cost economic catastrophe in society; a case in point, is the Republic of China having to be the primary financial lender to the United States; thus, boomed the economy of the United States in a short-run and simultaneously busted the economy for a long-run. Reinhart and Rogoff (2009) analysts of historical economic evidence asserted that boom typically precedes collapse just as "pride goes before a fall" p.118. They argued that demographic shifts may have caused most townships in local counties to dissipate or at the verge of dissipating if only adequate decisions in policies are initiated by the authorities that will protect the underlying risks from happening. Uzawa (2005), an endogenous growth theorist, was also interested in the relationship between economic growth and education. In contrast to Lucas, Uzawa saw endogenous growth as resulting from externalities based on the accumulation of human capital rather than on diminishing returns. Lucas's and Uzawa's models have some similarities, except that Uzawa did not take into account the externalities of human capital accumulation. For Lucas, human capital supersedes mere labor force participation rates. Uzawa, on the other hand, retains the classical notion of the non-reproducible labor factor. Azariadis and Drazen (2006) noted that Lucas's model has been a basis for other studies of how economic growth is affected by investment in education.

Solow (2000) argued that economic growth is not adequately accounted for by increases in capital and labor, asserting that technical progress must also be considered. Solow applied a simple linear regression model to economic analysis, which was consistent with Lucas's (1988) contention that training duration reflects the expansion of human resources. Lucas's test begins with a calculation of training duration, which is compared to school attendance. Several approximations are proposed in Lucas's test pattern: illiteracy rates, schooling levels, diplomas awarded, and annual average wages. Lucas's second stage involves measuring human capital by validating training. Results are adjusted to account for cost coefficients because years of schooling and number of diplomas are not equivalent. To validate results, Lucas proposed an additional estimate that assumes a correlation between annual wages and human capital.

Han and Suen (2009) proposed in their findings on industrial restructuring that industrial specific human capital is prone to reduce incentives for these categories of workers, such as: older workers, less educated workers who have less general human capital, and male workers that are leaving a declining industry. In the other hand, they inserted that incentives are raised for younger workers, well educated workers, and female workers that are willing to join growing industry. Hsieh and Woo (2005) supported the notion of Han and Suen (2009) and added that the average age of workers has risen by 42.1 years which is 3.9 years higher than the textile restructured industrial average at the time of the study. Freyer (2007) argued that there is significant correlation between the age structure of a workforce and productivity growth across industries. MacDonald and Weisbach (2004) indicated that technology changes tends to depreciate older workers skills and productivity as against younger worker who are purported to be better technologically, thus, priced higher in wages capacity in the same job description than older workers. Devereux (2006) asserted in their study of wage and mobility that workers who are movers due to non-expansion in growth in their industry are 20% to 25% higher than workers who are stayers in an expanding industry with much faster growth potential. Autor and Don (2009) supported MacDonald and Weisbach (2004) and Devereux (2006) assertions in their use of average of workers for occupational opportunities.

Han and Suen (2009) proposed that when industry retrenched their workers, efficient separation implies that the older workers that have accumulated more industrial specific human capital are less likely to be employed in another industry. On the other hand, younger workers of the same scenario will find a different job due to their greater incentive to invest in a new type of industry specific human capital. Shalla (2010) argued that older workers future are bleak due to age segmentation, constrained choices, lack of flexibility, increased income insecurity and disparity, and poverty. She also stated that older workers faced employment opportunities age discrimination, lower quality job descriptions to level of skills, reduced training prospects, increased health and injury risks and structural challenges that espouse younger workers ability to attain a quality position of management in the firm in place of the older workers. Fayrer (2009) argued that quality management affect productivity output and the scope of the firm. He used Lucas (1988) model in his investigation of quality management and productivity to assert that the quality of talented managers translates directly into the firms direct output. In other words, given the same quality of labor and capital, firms with quality managers produce more outputs. He also indicated that heterogeneity in management quality with a decrease in the return to scale will result to anarchy between the size of the firm and management talent. Feyrer analyses using Lucas framework resulted that baby boomers (older workers) in management structure are prone to lower management talents that directly affect productivity and parallel slowdown in United States productivity circle. Feyrer (2009) asserted that Kogel (2005) investigation on baby boomers in management also resulted in the same findings that older workers with lower management talents caused the overall drop in management quality that led to a total fall in productivity output.

Dimension of Population and Economic Formation

Chen (2006) asserted that a stochastic dynamic model is best suited for considering the effects of migration on economic growth. He used cross-sectional regression analysis to identify a dimension of population formation and the effects of economic growth. Yakita (2006) argued that an increase in longevity promotes savings, which is equal to capital investment and translates into economic growth. Empirical evaluations of Lucas's (1988) model have led to converging conclusions about the verifiability of endogenous growth and the relationships economic growth, population, and education. According to Benhabib and Spiegel (2004), human capital is a significant determinant on production, a conclusion that contradicts some theories of endogenous growth. Barro and Lee (2000) exploited the success of the new growth theories to confirm positive trends regarding human capital. For Solow (2000), a direct test of the endogenous growth hypothesis could be conducted only after the assumption testing advocated by Barro and Lee was accepted. Aghion and Howitt (2005) asserted that many studies took a careful look at the correlation between economic growth and population and arrived at their various conclusions that there is no relationship between the variables. However, Laincz and Peretto (2006) indicated that long-term economic growth rate is independent of scale due to endogenous product proliferation such as spillovers, composition effects, oligopolistic market behavior, fixed operating cost, research and development (R&D), trades, and endogenous population growth.

Laincz and Peretto (2006) asserted that with population dynamism, growth rate increases because the larger the labor force that are absorbed in the workforce, the more R&D over-time, and the larger the enterprise which is tantamount of causing spillover of workers to other new Firms in the demographical area. As a result, they concluded that transitional dynamics should be taken into consideration on growth and population relationship. Lucas (1988) asserted that human capital growth rates and training duration were negatively related. Lucas also indicated a negative relationship between training duration and increases in human capital; and growth is not affected strictly by human capital accumulation. However, this assumption seems at odds with Lucas's hypothesis that the growth of human capital is linear and limitless. He concluded that human capital, like other factors, is unlikely to break the law of diminishing returns. Dasgupta (2007) argued that although economic growth cannot buy happiness, it can lead to a better quality of life for citizens. Dasgupta asserted that growth in gross domestic product (GDP) per capita is commensurate with individual lifestyles and reflects the sustainability of economic development. Tonnessen (2008) concurred with Dasgupta's (2007) connecting population increase to GDP but argued that it is difficult to predict economic growth. Tonnessen claimed that although increased productivity can lead to economic growth, it can also have negative environmental consequences.

According to Dasgupta (2007), rich countries become rich because of their creative and innovative ideas, which lead to new products. Dasgupta argued that education, advances in science and technology, and incentives for growth and development are essential for steady economic growth. He noted that some areas with recent population increases have experienced declines in real gross domestic product per capita. Duesterberg (2007) noted that long-term growth potential is equal to population size plus productivity. Duesterberg countered that declining fertility rates, increased mechanized agriculture, and greater manufacturing productivity are what affect economic growth. He also argued that the spread of wealth and education in advanced societies contributes to lower fertility rates.

Maestas and Zissimopoulos (2010) asserted that the effects of an aging population have not reached an alarming stage that some theorists predicted. Nevertheless, they predicted that challenges will arise when there is an increase in the elderly population and a decline in the younger generation, with the result that consumption patterns will outpace productive capacity. Maestas and Zissimopoulos argued that the impact of an aging population on a society's standard of living will depend on the average retirement age. They predicted that changes in employer-provided pensions and Social Security are likely to propel increases in labor force participation at older ages. They are optimistic for the future economy because the labor market is accommodating elderly workers to some degree, which could substantially lessen the negative economic impact of an aging population.

Prettner and Prskawetz (2010) noted that investing in the human capital of children, suggests that lower fertility prompts higher investments in education and correspondently higher per capita output. They noted that although human capital depreciates as people begin forgetting what they previously knew, job training (learning by doing) can enhance young workers' skills over time. Guest, Shacklock, and Skirbekk studied redistribution effects between age groups and observed that mature workers and their younger counterparts have differing attributes.

> Younger workers tend to have better physical strength and endurance, vision, hearing, cognitive processing, intellectual capital, and adaptability, whereas mature workers are perceived as having better people management skills, judgment that depends on experience, reliability, dependability, loyalty, and attendance (as cited in Prettner & Prskawetz, 2010, p. 208).

These researchers predicted that any change in workforce age structure will affect intergenerational wage distribution as a result of demographic developments that prompt labor supply changes, specifically human capital resources of mature versus young workers.

Mitchell and Mosler (2006) asserted that environmental sustainability is important for economic growth. They argued that environmental policies must accompany attempts to stimulate capital formation in both private and public sectors in both local and regional economies. They also recommended public investment in higher education to help create a foundation for private investment. Blanchard and Matthew (2006) noted that globalization influences civic participation in local communities, which is affected by the problem-solving mechanism embedded in local businesses. They argued that unlike large absentee corporations that are exposed to global economic fluctuations, locally owned businesses enjoy pluralistic political structures that reflect both their civic and corporate relationships. Blanchard and Matthew postulated that civic communities involved in a network of associations that are considered the problem-solving mechanism for both the corporate and community welfare, they owe due diligence to the corporation rather than to the community because of the corporation's influence on economic activities in the community; such as financial support and decision power to relocate their goods and services if their policies or reform efforts are resisted. They further argued that the influence of multinational corporations endowed with broad decision-making power has caused deterioration of local civic engagement in population and may deter long-term economic growth in a community.

Regional and Equity Theoretical Model

Sertich's (2004) framework for regional governance uses institutions of higher education as catalysts for social change. Sertich described the formation of the Northeast Higher Education District (NHED), which is made up of five colleges. NHED's mission is:

> to provide higher education to communities in northeastern Minnesota by developing a regional structure that aligns programs and services to better prepare residents for learning, employment, citizenship, and life. A unique extension of that mission is the district's active engagement in creating a more robust regional economy. In particular, the college's five campuses work to promote effective relationships with each community, providing services to business and industry as well as creating ties with state and regional economic development initiatives. (Sertich, 2004, pp. 58-59)

Sertich (2004) described five foundations for a healthy economy: "government, health and social services, education and training, community infrastructure, and the economy itself" (p. 58). He argued that governance should balance these components by providing uniform access, regardless of where a community is located. NHED created partnerships with local governments and businesses. The result was "a new commitment to the future of the region' (Sertich, 2004, p. 59), symbolized in a new brand name (True North) that "describes cooperation among higher education, the private sector, and government: the three points of a figurative arrowhead" (p. 59). True North undertook additional meetings with government and private-sector and leaders to spread the new vision.

> Its first major economic initiative was the TechNorth Prep Center Network, a system of work sites that matches students seeking training and experience with businesses seeking young talent. Participants include start-up businesses,

back-office contract service providers, and larger established organizations. This broad spectrum of tenants illustrates the fresh linkages the center has sought in the community. (Sertich, 2004, p. 59)

The coalition stressed interdependence among governmental and nongovernmental entities. True North especially targeted rural areas in crafting and implementing new economic development strategies. The emphasis was on good governance, which involves "engaging people in a democratic process and giving them the opportunity to be included in how decisions are made" (Sertich, 2004, p. 60). Good governance gives a voice to the disenfranchised, crosses boundaries (political districts, county lines), builds and sustains coalitions, seeks meaningful social and economic outcomes, and applies lessons from the past to future plans (Sertich, 2004).

According to Power (as cited in Sertich, 2004), "research universities should play a leading role in helping rural regions reinvent their economies" (p. 62). Jischke (as cited in Sertich, 2004) argued that:

> the most effective development of knowledge-based economies is happening in states and regions that partner with research universities and Purdue University aims to do the same for Indiana, according to Power. In response to the recent economic downturn, partnerships were formed among Indiana businesses, government, and research universities to identify sectors in the state with the greatest promise for future economic growth. Purdue is taking the lead by supporting these areas with new investments in science and technology. (p. 63)

Power (as cited in Sertich, 2004) stated that "to help Indiana tap the knowledge economy, Purdue's efforts are becoming interdisciplinary and multi-institutional" (p. 63). The university "recognizes that barriers often exist among academic disciplines and is working to eliminate them" (p. 63). This initiative will enable researchers across disciplines to establish new programs for the ever-changing knowledge economy.

> Purdue's Discovery Park is a cluster of research centers that connects faculty and students from many disciplines.

> Research is resulting in the development of market-ready technologies . . . Centers on e-enterprise, biomedical engineering, and cancer research is on the horizon. Discovery Park is aimed at fostering growth throughout all of Indiana, and rural areas have much to gain. Technology incubators could translate into new high-tech businesses locating in rural Indiana. (Sertich, 2004, pp. 63-64)

Power (as cited in Sertich, 2004) indicated that Indiana farmers have already profited from research that developed disease-resistant soybeans. The state's timber industry has benefited by the development of new species of trees. Rural businesses have access to Purdue's Technical Assistance Program, which provides assistance with the everyday issues associated with managing a business and developing new products. (p. 64).

Salmonson (as cited in Sertich, 2004) noted that cooperative arrangements of this type require that participants share ideas freely. Change advocates are also important for new initiatives. Whitaker (as cited in Sertich, 2004) described champions as "those who take risks and accept the consequences" (p. 69). Welty (as cited in Sertich, 2004) identified seven components that are needed for rural regions to thrive:

1. A sense of place.
2. Engagement by higher education.
3. An entrepreneurial culture.
4. Collaboration and cooperation among regional leaders.
5. Financial investment from multiple institutions.
6. Strong leadership; organizational and economic infrastructure.
7. Educational and training programs that serve the region's goals. (p. 69).

Summary

A dearth of research on how to address population decline in rural areas led to the present study: an analysis of the economic prospects of Pierce County, North Dakota. The purpose of the NHED study was to create a model that will help local communities balance population control with long-term economic growth.

CHAPTER 3

Methodological Approach on Population and Economic Growth

A rationale for choosing a mixed-methods approach for the analysis of examining the effect of population decline on the economic growth of a Northern County in US was to present a combination of quantitative (documents, survey) and qualitative (interviews) methods that will best serve in describing the setting, population, sample, data collection and analysis procedures, and steps taken for the ethical protection of participants.

Quantitative Design Initiatives

According to Wang and Zhou (2009), quantitative study is the scientific examination of properties and their relationship. The goal of some quantitative research is to develop a mathematical model and hypotheses from converted numbers and data. Measurement is crucial to quantitative studies because it provides an essential connection between empirical observation and mathematical expression. Nielson (2004) noted that although quantitative approaches are sometimes narrow, they help researchers maintain focus and objectivity. According to Hagan (2000), the quantitative approach is attractive because of its ability to provide precise results. Singleton and Straits (2005) argued that quantitative study is consistent with the scientific method. It is noted that quantitative research dominates the hard sciences but that in the social sciences qualitative studies have become common.

To confirm population decline, U.S. Census records, as well as county records on school enrollment was conducted. County records were used to determine economic trends. These records included taxable valuation and tax levies, statements of revenues, expenditures, transfers, and fund balances and final budget in the US Northern county.

The Population and Economic Growth (PEG) survey was administered (see Appendix A), to 25 participants in a US Northern County. The survey collected some demographic data (gender, type of employment, age) and participants' impressions of population and economic trends in the County. The survey asked what types of tax data are used to measure the county's economic status; whether the county's population, mortality rate, and fertility rate are increasing or decreasing; whether elderly residents are adequately prepared for retirement; and whether locating a 2-year college in the county is desirable.

Qualitative Design Initiatives

For Creswell (2007), qualitative research is a process that involves solving human problems in a natural setting while maintaining sensitivity to the people and places under study. He added that qualitative research entails understanding the context in which participants address an issue or problem. Researchers using qualitative methods attempt "to make sense of phenomena in terms of the meanings people bring to them" (p. 37). Qualitative research is especially useful in developing new theories when inadequate or partial explanations are all that exist to account for certain phenomena or populations.

According to Creswell and Lincoln (2005), qualitative inquiry is a naturalistic approach. Bailey (2007) described the qualitative approach as an attempt to examine social phenomena using sociological paradigms. According to Pope and Mays (2005), qualitative research has its roots in socio-philosophical paradigm. Hatch (2002) listed several specific strategies that qualitative researchers employ: examining documents, observing behavior, and interviewing informants.

Face-to-face semi-structured interviews were used to encourage a free flow of conversation with participants (see Appendix B). Creswell (2007) stated that a well-designed questionnaire is crafted with the most useful information to answer the research questions. Bailey (1987) noted that interviews enable researchers to probe for more specific information. Weiss and Fine (2000) and Numkoosing

(2005) encouraged interviewers to reflect on the dynamics of power and resistance, of consent and projection. The original intention was to use the survey questions as a starting point for individual interviews, to tape-record those interviews and prepare transcripts, and to subject those transcripts to coding for themes. In scheduling interviews, participants do not have to have their comments recorded. As an alternative strategy, interviewees answered their survey questions in writing that probed follow-up questions for more detailed responses.

Case Study Research Initiatives

According to Creswell (2007), "case study research involves the study of an issue through one or more cases within a bounded system." (p. 93). Case studies are appropriate when a study's goals depend on the nature of the setting and on participants' interests, needs, and point of view. Case studies are commonly used in sociology, psychology, medicine, law, and political science. Browne (2005) noted that one criticism of case studies is their focus on process over product. Supporters contend that the case study is based on an interpretative view of research and inquiry that acknowledges that no one reality can be specified except through generalizing (Tyler, 2000). As Creswell (2007) observed,

> There is no standard format for reporting case study research. Unquestionably, some case studies generate theory, some are simply descriptive, and others are more analytical in nature and display cross-case or inter-site comparisons. The overall intent of the case study undoubtedly shapes the larger structure of the written narrative. (p. 195)

This study's case study had the following characteristics:

1. The US Northern County was the unit of analysis, and a subset of its residents constituted the sample.
2. The study was bounded by time (1 month of data collection) and place (The specific US Northern County).
3. I used several sources of information in data collection to provide an in-depth picture of the population.
4. I devoted considerable attention to the context of the research.

Mixed-Methods Research Initiatives

Mixed-methods research involves the use of both qualitative and quantitative methods (Goldner, 2007). Creswell (2007) listed four research components that should be considered in deciding whether quantitative or qualitative methods will predominate: priority, implementation, integration, and theoretical perspective. Prioritizing involves establishing research goals and deciding which are most important. Implementation involves establishing a specific sequence of research methods, for example, a survey followed by interview questions that explore themes identified in the quantitative portion. Integration refers to how different types of data are combined. Theoretical perspectives are the ideas behind the research. Creswell noted that mixed-methods studies are common in medical research, where securing funding is easier if a proposed study has a quantitative element but where qualitative methods enable researchers to tap the human element. He described the mixed-method approach as an effective way to exploit both inductive and the deductive thinking. Quantitative research privileges deduction, where it is assumed that a conclusion is justified if the evidence is accurate. With induction, on the other hand, a conclusion may be uncertain even if the evidence is true because there is a reality that goes beyond the facts at hand, an assumption congenial to qualitative methods (Singleton & Straits, 2005).

Babbie (2007) observed that the quantitative approach is limited because it is sometimes difficult to equate human issues with other phenomena through a mathematical equation. He also stated that numerical findings are not always sufficient for solving problems that are sociological in nature. Creswell (2007) noted that qualitative research can be used along with quantitative research in solving research problems.

In discussing how researchers go about selecting a method, Hammersley (1996) described two paradigms: loyalty and methodological eclecticism. Hammersley argued that one should be loyal to a particular method unless that loyalty "denies a methodological eclecticism that may be useful" (p. 160). Hammersley saw the developing interest in mixed-methods research as "a solution to the artificial tensions created between qualitative and quantitative approaches" (pp. 165-170).

Research Setting and Sample Implications

The US Northern County had in 2008 a population of 4,091, down from 4,463 in 2003, and a population density of five people per square mile (cite). Over 98% of the population is White. The per capita income for the county in 2000 was $14,055. In 2009 the unemployment rate was 4.1%, compared to 3.2% in North Dakota as a whole. About 7% of the county's 2005 resident taxpayers moved to other counties in 2006 (City Data, 2010).

The sample consisted of 50 participants. Criterion sampling was used to select residents of both farming and non-farming communities in and around the three County towns. Participants selected were long-term residents of those communities who were likely to be knowledgeable about the area where they lived.

Participants were all 18 years of age and older. Fifty participants received mailed surveys with return envelopes. The researcher selected an additional 15 participants for individual interviews. According to Singleton and Straits (2005), there is no universally agreed-upon criterion for selecting interviewees. The researcher chose people who were especially knowledgeable about the area.

Instrumentation and Material Implications

A mixed-methods approach was used that included documents, a survey (see Appendix A), and semi-structured interviews (see Appendix B). The researcher designed the Population and Economic Growth Survey (PEGS) specifically for this case study and pilot tested it with 15 participants. The PEGS consists of 13 multiple-choice and short-answer questions; in the final phase it was administered to 25 participants. The survey used in this study was designed to take advantage of the SPSS Guttman scaling response format, which enables a researcher to assess respondents' knowledge and opinions about a broad range of topics (Singleton & Straits, 2005, p. 275). Table 1 shows the relationship between survey-interview items and the study's research questions.

Table 1

Relationship Between Research Questions and Survey-Interview Questions

Research question	Interview/survey question
What is the correlation between population decline and economic growth?	2, 3, 4, 5, 9, 10, 11, 12, 13
What impact has population decline had on employment?	3, 4, 5, 9, 10, 11, 12, 13
What effect has education development had on economic growth?	4, 5, 10, 11, 12, 13
What impact has population decline had on the elderly population?	1, 2, 3, 7, 10, 13

Interview questions were based on the PEGS and were designed to give participants an opportunity to provide additional details about their experience. The researcher interviewed 10 participants for an average of 15 minutes each. Interviews were conducted in participants' workplaces. Interviews were not tape-recorded; instead, I took detailed notes during each interview. Interview results were reviewed by participants at the end of each interview, and amendments were incorporated into the final version.

Reliability and Validity Implications

To determine the reliability of the PEGS, a pilot study was conducted with 15 participants. These respondents were not part of the sample used in the final study. Babbie (2007) indicated that interview questions are reliable when they are easy to understand by respondents and relevant to the subject under discussion.

The total population sample ($N = 35$) included equal numbers of men and women. The farming business accounted for 58% of respondents, compared to 41% for non-farming business. The highest percentage of participants (42%) fell in the 35-49 categories, and the lowest percentage (3%) was in the 18-34 categories.

The majority of respondents (60%) chose sales tax as the principal source of revenue in the Northern County. Most participants (81%) said the population is declining. Among the reasons they listed for decline were that the Northern County is an agricultural county, economies of scale for farmers, and migration of residents to bigger towns and cities in search of knowledge-based careers. A majority of respondents (56%) rated Northern County's economic growth as 7 in a scale of 10. They said that attracting manufacturing jobs to the county and reeducating the labor force (farmers and high school graduates) through technical education will contribute to stable economic growth.

The baby boomers are between the ages of 35 and 65 and younger adults are between the ages of 18 to 34. The county's median age still remains below 34. As observed, migration to the county has remained insignificant, resulting in a 0.5% increase in the school population between 2007 and 2008. This increase resulted in a 0.1% growth in revenue, as shown in Table 3. As the county's population ages, there may be serious long-term implications for the economy. Kinghorn and Justis (2008) posed that rural counties face the challenge of aging populations that are expected to slow economic growth. This assertion raises the question of whether there is a correlation between the variables and the effect it will have on long-term economic growth. The main reliability test that will formulate the results of the linear relationship of the variables is based on the two-tailed t test that indicated if the regression slope is equals zero. Conversely, if the slope does not equal zero, the two variables have a linear relationship. The test used to determine rejection and non-rejection of the null hypothesis is as follows: $t^{(n-2)} = b1 - (\beta_1)_0 / s\,(b_1)$. This formula calculates Estimate — Hypothesized parameter value / Standard error of estimator.

The ability of the tests to differentiate the probability of the outcomes based on the analysis of the data will prove the validity of the dimension of the study. Even though the dimensions of the data can be manipulated, the responses of the participants and reliability of the survey in conjunction with the SPSS analysis, all the dimensions have been procured to create a reliable result. The finding will support the significance of the correlation of the variables under investigation.

The narratives provided by the participants with high percentages of the responses in all demographic groups indicate that targeted population intended to become more informed and discerning with regard to what they are confronted with in the context of the PEG. Furthermore, comparisons of the results from the research designs show noticeable differences in the interpretation. However, due to the level of sophistication of the participants concerned, and the importance of the overall integrity of the study, it is noted that, in keeping with Creswell (2007), the primary concerns of reliability are consistency, stability, and repeatability. Singleton and Straits (2005) listed three ways to assess an instrument's reliability:

1. Repeated applicability of the measure (test-retest reliability).
2. Responses to subsets of items from the same measure (split-half reliability).
3. Examining the consistency of responses across all items (internal consistency).

Pilot Study Implications

Schwab (2005) recommended pilot testing a survey with participants who have similar knowledge to those who will be asked to complete the instrument as a part of the final study. Schwab asserted that this procedure will help a researcher identify mistaken assumptions about participants' frame of reference and target items that are difficult to understand. Selitz et al. (2005) argued that pilot test often will lead to changes in the survey questionnaire and may increase response rates, reduce missing data, and yield more valid responses on the final questionnaire. Selitz asserted that for a self-designed survey questionnaire to be reliable, it is important to test the instrument through a pilot study.

A pilot test helps the researcher identify misguided assumptions about participants' frame of reference and target survey items that are difficult to understand. The goal of pilot testing is to improve response rates, reduce missing data, and prompt a greater number of valid responses on the final version of the questionnaire.

To enhance the reliability of the PEGS, the researcher pilot tested the survey with 15 participants in the same target population. In addition to administering the survey, the researcher solicited participants' reactions to the wording and perceived intent of each item. The process was conversational and was conducted in a low-key manner so as not to intimidate or overburden respondents. The survey begins with demographic information—age, gender, type of business—in order to determine eligibility for participation and to route respondents through subsequent sections of the survey. The results of the tests were used to modify the survey instrument and interview questions and thus, revised the original survey by simplifying some items.

It is worthwhile to mention that in conducting the pilot test, the researcher followed procedures recommended by Peat, Mellis, Williams, and Xuan (2002):

1. Administer the questionnaire to pilot participants in exactly the same way as it will be administered in the main study.
2. Ask participants for feedback to identify ambiguities and difficult questions.
3. Record the time taken to complete the questionnaire and decide whether it is reasonable.
4. Discard all unnecessary, difficult, or ambiguous questions.
5. Assess whether each question gives an adequate range of responses.
6. Confirm that replies can be interpreted in terms of the information required.
7. Check that all questions are answered.
8. Reword or rescale any questions that are not answered as expected (p. 123).

Although the survey is a well-established method of data collection in social science research, constructing a survey is by no means an exact science. To help ensure that a survey is understandable and measures what it is intended to measure, researchers recommend administering a pilot study to test an instrument's intelligibility, utility, and reliability.

Research Questions and Hypotheses Implications

This study was based on four research questions:

1. What is the correlation between population decline and economic growth in the US Northern County?
2. What impact has population decline had on employment in the US Northern County?
3. What effect has educational development had on economic growth in the US Northern County?
4. What impact has population decline had on the elderly population in the US Northern County?

These questions generated two hypotheses:

H_o: A decline in population will affect economic growth.
H_1: A decline in population will not affect economic growth.

I tested the hypotheses using Aczel and Sounderpandian's (2006) recommendations:

1. Specify the level of significance (alpha).
2. Determine the sample size (n).
3. Specify the critical values that divide the rejection and nonrejection regions.
4. Determine the test statistics.
5. Enter the data and compute the sample value of the test statistics.
6. Determine the statistical decisions or results (p. 283).

The Data Collection Implications

Interviewing and observation played a significant role in this study. Other forms of data collected were participants' observation, participants' memos taking during the unstructured open-ended interviews, and documents in form of analyzed public records. These sources of this approach were recommended by several reearchers (Creswell, 2007; Hammersley & Atkinson, 1995; Spradley, 1979, 1980). Quantitative surveys, tests, and measures are part of the data collection incorporated in this research process. Asmussen and Creswell, (1995) used similar forms of data collection as a way of bringing clarity in an information-rich case study. Najdowski et al., in their study on behavior change on children with pervasive development disorder, asserted that the primary method to assess credible research is through repeated data collection.

As a process of the in-depth techniques conducted in the data collected, the researcher reviewed a variety of documents to determine population and economic trends in the US Northern County. The researcher analyzed U.S. Census records, as well as county records on school enrollment. The researcher also used county records on taxable valuation and tax levies in North Dakota cities; statements of revenues, expenditures, transfers, final budget figures, and fund balances pertaining to the US Northern County. Census data covered the period from 1960 to 2000, the last year for which census data are available. Pierce County records covered the period from 1997 to 2008.

The researcher used purposeful, non-proportional, criterion sampling to select 50 participants residing in three US Northern County communities. Singleton and Straits (2005) recommended purposeful sampling when a researcher is knowledgeable about the population under study and well-qualified to choose reliable participants. Participants came from both farming and non-farming regions. All were 18 years of age or older. Of the 50 County residents invited to participate in the study, 25 completed a consent form and returned a completed survey, for a response rate of 50%.

The researcher targeted additional 15 County residents for individual interviews. The researcher was able to schedule and conduct interviews with 10 of these. At the request of interviewees, the researcher did not record interviews. Participants responded in writing to the interview questions, which were the same questions used in the survey. The researcher used those written responses as prompts for follow-up questions to elicit more detailed and revealing responses. The researcher emulated Asmussen and Creswell's (1995) case study structure on "campus response to a student gunman" (p. 92) in preparing the data collection process for this study. The researcher also added personnel perception with regards to designing the PEG survey with a focus on the targeted population. Since this case is a bounded system, and is bounded by 3 months of data collection, it provided a detailed, in-depth picture of the demography of the County as indicated in the study's tables and figures. Thus, with this data, a constructed picture of the conceptualized case was attained and the reactions were noted through several themes that assisted in the formulation of the results.

The next phase of the information gathering process was the interpretation and analyzing of the data which involves the lessons derived from the data collected. Creswell (2007), Lincoln and Guba (1985, 2000) and Stake (1995) indicated interpretation is based on hunches, insights, and intuitions. The forms of interpretations are categorical aggregation, direct interpretation, patterns, and naturalistic generalizations. The researcher chose the naturalistic generalizations for its interpretation and analytic phenomenon based on Lincoln and Guba's, Stake's, and Creswell's assertions that by analyzing the data one can learn from the case and apply the concept to the population of other cases. Thus, starting with the raw data collected, The researcher categorized the data into several specific and general themes (categorized aggregation) that were coded for the purpose of easy interpretation. The case hypotheses were stated to specify the relationships among various categories of the information gathered. Finally, SPSS was used to analyze the coded themes from one domain to another for a later feedback of results.

The Data Analysis Implications

The objective of the researcher was to investigate the relationship between population decline and economic growth. He used purposeful sampling to collect data on the perceptions of the targeted population sample (N = 25). A self-designed Population and Economic Growth Survey (PEGS) is in Appendix A. The targeted participants represented both farming and non-farming occupations. The self-designed PEGS comprise of 13 items. According to Creswell (2007), qualitative and qualitative data can be gathered at the same time, if possible.

The data analysis included the use of descriptive statistics. Aczel and Sounderpandian (2006) asserted that descriptive statistics is a science that can assist in making improved decisions in summarizing and analyzing data. The ANOVA analysis and the t test were also used to confirm the multicollinearity of the data. To analyze the reliability of participants' responses, an adapted Guttman scale SPSS open code and qualitative frequencies were used. Huberman and Wiles (1994) supported the use of general data analysis strategies that make contrasts and comparisons, highlight and identify codes, and determine frequencies that are commonly used in qualitative research analysis.

The researcher reviewed population figures, including census data and school enrollment figures, to determine population and economic growth trends in the US Northern County. Results of the PEGS were determined by creating summary statistics. Percentages were computed for gender and age breakdown, as well as participants' impression of whether the County population, mortality rate, and fertility rate are increasing or declining. The researcher computed mean, median, and mode statistics for the item that asked participants to assign a numerical score to economic growth in Pierce County.

The PEGS was formulated using the following 10 dimensions:

1. Education: diversity of knowledge.
2. Immigration: incoming skills.
3. Emigration: outgoing skills (brain drain).
4. Employment: pertinent to development and growth.
5. Elderly residents: predominant in bounded population.
6. Long-term economic growth: stability in development.
7. Fertility: increase in birth rate.
8. Mortality: decrease in death rate
9. Human capital: paradigm of investment.
10. Advanced technology: protégé for innovation and diversity.

The researcher used simple linear regression analysis to determine the correlation coefficient between population and economic growth. Aczel and Sounderpandian (2006) asserted that a simple linear regressive model is considered the best analysis regarding correlation coefficients. The following conditions were adhered to:

1. When the correlation coefficient (p) is equal to 0, there is no correlation.
2. When the correlation coefficient (p) is equal to 1, there is a perfect positive correlation. That is, when the independent variable increases, the dependent variable also increases, and when the independent variable decreases, the dependent variable also decreases.

3. When the correlation coefficient (p) is equal to -1, there is a perfect negative correlation between the two variables. That is, when the independent variable increases, the dependent variable decreases, or when the independent variable decreases, the dependent variable increases.
4. When the absolute value of a correlation coefficient (p) is 0 or 1, it reflects the relative strength of the relationship between variables. For example, 0.80 indicates a relatively strong positive correlation; -0.60 indicates a weaker, negative correlation; 0.20 implies a relatively weak positive correlation or linear relationship (Aczel & Sounderpandian, 2006, p. 448).

To account for random error (e) that might emerge during statistical calculations, it is necessary to test whether the independent and dependent variables are correlated, using the hypothesis test of Ho: p = 0; H1: p = 0 (Aczel & Sounderpandian, 2006, pp. 451-452). This test shows a validation of the null hypothesis that assumes zero correlation.

After the interviews were completed, the researcher coded the results. Creswell (2007) described coding as a process whereby nonnumeric data are reconstituted into numerical data. In coding, the followed steps were adopted:

1. Read notes and created interview transcripts.
2. Selected a specific interview record for analysis.
3. Created abbreviations for topics and wrote out codes next to the opposite data.
4. Located the descriptive phrases in the data and developed them into categories.
5. Outlined the information.

Themes that emerged during the analysis included emigration, employment, the elderly and long-term economic growth. In the data transformation process, the researcher counted all the times a specific theme surfaced. The purpose was to establish correlations between variables. Creswell (2007) described this process as facilitating quantitative decisions with qualitative data.

According to Creswell (2007) the concept of purposeful sampling entails that the researcher will selects participants and sites for the study because the participants have proper knowledge of the population and they can purposefully understand the research problems and the central phenomenon in the study. The researcher will make the decisions about who and what will be sampled, the criteria of the sampling format, how many people or sites will be involved in the sampling process, and if the sampling will be consistent with the case study approach. Marshall and Rossman (2006) asserted that sampling can change during a study and researcher needs to be flexible.

Creswell (2007) regarded case study as a bridge across a paradigm that can generate theory, describe cases, and reflect a cross-case comparisons between two variables. The researcher proposition is that case study theory is rhetorical in nature due to the fact that if an individual has related thoughts or perceptions, his or her main focus is how to source the objectives and solve for or restoring valued consistency to the perceptions. Stake (2006) noted that an individual can open or close a case study narrative with vignettes to draw the reader to a case.

Participants' Sensitivity Initiatives

In any research involving human subjects, researchers must be sensitive to the needs of vulnerable populations. They must avoid exploiting unbalanced power relations and placing participants at risk (Creswell, 2007). Throughout the data collection process, the researcher was able to ensure that participants were treated with the utmost respect and decorum. Each participant signed a consent form before volunteering any information. The researcher explained the purpose of the study to all participants. They were assured that all their responses would be kept confidential and that no penalty would result if they chose to withdraw from the study at any time.

Summary

In this chapter, the researcher described the methods used for a mixed-method case study of 35 residents of the County, based on documents, a survey and interviews. The researcher described data collection and analysis procedures, and steps taken for the ethical protection of participants. In the following chapter, The researcher also presented the results of the study.

CHAPTER 4

Research Instrumentation Initiatives

The results of the study, addressed both the quantitative (documents, survey) and qualitative (interviews) portions of the research. The dependent variables examined were employment, education, human capital, technology, innovation, and economic growth. The independent variables were emigration, mortality rate, fertility rate, elderly needs, and population decline. Participants represented both farming and non-farming occupations.

The self-designed PEGS comprised 13 items. Choices were *yes*, *no*, *all of the above*, and *not sure*. The written PEGS were administered to 25 participants, and the PEGS were used as the basis for face-to-face interviews with an additional 10 participants. Creswell (2007) noted that case studies are typically less specialized and less regimented than some forms of quantitative research. The period under study was 1960-2008. U.S. census data were available only from 1960 to 2000. The 2010 census results will not be available until 2011. In addition to census data, the researcher used public domain and official records for the County. These documents included information on school enrollment, as well as county revenues and expenditures. School population data reflected the pattern of population decline in the County. Singleton and Straits (2005) noted that comparable data sources can be used to confirm the reliability of individual sources in the same targeted population.

Research Documentations

According to U.S. Census data, the population of the US Northern County has declined steadily, from 7,394 in 1960 to 4,675 in 2000 (see Table 2).

Table 2

Pierce County Population

Year	Population
1960	7,394
1970	6,483
1980	6,252
1990	5,052
2000	4,675

Note. From Pierce County Office of Archives and Population Census, Office of the Auditor, 2008.

From 1997 to 2008, the school age population saw an overall decline, from 775 in 1997 to 567 in 2008. The last 2 years for which data are available show a slight increase (see Table 3).

Table 3

Pierce County School Enrollment

Year	School Enrollment
1997	775
1998	754
1999	743
2000	665
2001	644
2002	606
2003	587
2004	563
2005	547
2006	531
2007	560
2008	567

Note. From Pierce County Schools, Office of the Superintendent.

The US Northern County's annual statement of revenues, expenditures, and fund balances from 1997 to 2007 reveals modest overall economic growth (see Table 4).

Table 4

Pierce County Revenues, Expenditures, and FYE Fund Balances 1997-2007

Year	Beginning fund balance	Revenues	Expenditures	Ending fund balance
1997	$276.936.65	$732.996.52	$667,477.87	$342,455.30
1998	$342,455.30	$771,212.08	$689,576.21	$424,091.07
1999	$424,091.07	$827,320.73	$681,020.10	$570,391.80
2000	$570,391.80	$862,371.91	$681,306.87	$751,456.84
2001	$751,456.84	$854,004.23	$719,910.75	$885,550.32
2002	$885,550.32	$794,935.07	$733,082.04	$896,882.04
2003	$896,882.04	$828,271.73	$698,084.34	$1,027,069.43
2004	$1,027,069.43	$781,736.91	$740,533.43	$1,018,272.91
2005	$1,018,272.91	$773,905.73	$822,739.91	$969,438.73
2006	$969,438.73	$895,350.03	$835,366.45	$1,029,422.31
2007	$1,029,422.31	$921,653.27	$845,365.59	$1,105,709.99

Sampling Selection Initiatives

A complete case analysis method was used to select participants who were assumed to be representative sample of the targeted population. The participants' covariance of interest is not in any way distorted in the sample compared to that of the targeted population. Thus, the case sample selection was based on estimation and the knowledge base composition of the participants in the targeted population demography. On the other hand, it can be argued that the factor of inducing participants' selection using a purposeful approach can be considered a bias factor.

According to Binder (1992) and Lin (2000), as cited by Pan and Schaubel (2009), Inverse-Selection-Probability-Weighting (ISPW) can be used to select participants based on their knowledge of the targeted population. Pan and Schaubel (2008) also proposed an inference procedure of weighting participants based on an empirical method, while Kasprzyk et al. (1989) suggested that empirically weighted estimator gain a better efficiency relatively to an unweighted estimator because the weighted participants are knowledgeable on the targeted population to select for the sample. In the current study, the reliability and the validity of the pilot study testing played a critical role in the sample selection process.

Pan and Schaubel (2008) indicated that in the presence of a potentially biased sample data, it is better to compare the weighted and the unweighted parameter of sample estimates. They proposed a regression parameter for a single test such that only one model of either weighted or unweighted method can be chosen for sample selection. I used a weighted model method for sample selection due its efficiency and its richness in gathering data.

The sampling selection was geared towards predicting the correlation of variables and other distinct issues relating to the desirability of the research and the research questions. The challenge imposed by the sample selection process was the integration and the comparative weighting of the sampling designs. The results from the sample selection were consistent with cross-regression analyses of the survey data and the quantitative data that formulated estimations of the findings for interpretation.

Collection and Conversion of Data

Quantitative data were provided by County government officials as well as through a survey of the researcher's design. Qualitative data consisted of personal interview responses. The data were collected by structuring the argument of the study around the framework of preference measurement comprising three interrelated components. The first component is the problems the study is intended to address. The second component is the task of the design that focuses on the data collection approach. The third and final component is the specification and estimate of the preference model that relates to the conversion of the data into the action. Netzer et al. (2008) indicated that this type of framework has been viewed by researchers as mostly the method of choice for quantitative and qualitative preference measurement. Thus, the preference measurement data have been collected using questionnaires and interviews involving sorting, rating tasks, and theme coding. Gustafsson et al. (2007) posited that the context of the conjoint analysis is a paradigm for the field of preference measurement that remains vital in data collection phenomenon, such as problem solving, preferences among hypothesis profiles, and the conversion of the analyzed data into action.

The data collection was based on knowledge of the demography, whereby the participants were purported to be knowledgeable of the targeted population. Open interactions were encouraged between the respondents and the researcher during the interview process. Netzer et al. (2008) argued that in formulating a data collection mechanism, it is important to note the experience of the respondents or participants completing the tasks. In addition, I the respondents to narrate freely where asked in the designed questionnaire instead of the use of audio taping that was rejected by the respondents. Netzer et al. (2008) indicated that preference measurement can be used in interdisciplinary studies. Gilbride and Allenby (2004) and Kohli and Jedidi (2007) used preference measurement techniques to study formation of consideration sets designed to guide project selection and investment decisions. Saigal et al. (2007) used conjoint analysis to optimize treatment for prostate cancer based on each patient's unique situations and side effects. Tanaka et al. (2007) studied relationships among parameters that represented loss or risk aversion and individual characteristics such as age, income, and education. Fehr and Goette (2007) and Jamebrant et al. (2008) studied parameters and behavior in advances in preference measurement in questionnaire designs.

Michalek et al. (2005) used the prior knowledge of respondents' preferences, as in the present study, to facilitate the design stage of a preference measurement. Sandor and Wedel (2005) argued that prior knowledge about heterogeneity of respondents' preferences are efficient and affect design optimality. Netzer et al. (2008) suggested that preference measurement is flexible and typically assumes linear and adaptive utility functions. It should also be noted that statistical and optimization methods were used at the final stage of the preference measurement to give a clear model of population stabilization with long-term economic growth.

Survey Participants' Demographic Classifications

The participant demographic classification of this research survey entails the farming and non-farming population of the US Northern County. This information was needed for this study because of the likely degree of participation that each of the participants was willing to give. Participants were required to fluently speak and write English. There were no educational requirements to participate in the survey; however, there was a residency requirement. Participants were required to live in the County and be knowledgeable about the communities that made up the County. According to Todd and Davis (1994), the best stimulant to entice participation is to allow participants to make a voluntary decision either to participate or not to participate in the survey. Todd and Davis asserted that the participants have to be knowledgeable and be satisfied with the contents of a survey.

Survey Design Initiatives

Some of the studies that are relevant in the review of literatures concentrated mostly on population and economic growth that led to the survey design are those by Dasgupter (2007); Groth, Koch, and Steger (2010); Zhuang and St. Juliana (2010); Yakita (2006); Lucas (1988); and Lee and Mason (2010). These endogenous theorists found that innovative ideas, education level, and advance in science and technology were best predictors of population stabilization and long-term economic growth. Groth, Koch, and Steger (2010) used the R&D based growth model and the semi-endogenous growth framework to measure and estimate the determinants of long-term per capita and the labor force growth rates that accommodated exponential growth with zero population.

Zhuang and St. Juliana (2010) explored high capital accumulation with capital production. They found that such capital intensiveness in a demographic area may result to a high propensity of accelerated economic growth and development. Zhuang and St. Juliana asserted that investment in human capital, technological advancement, and R&D will contribute to highly educated workforce that tends to improve on productivity and economic growth in both short and long-run. Yakita (2006) and Lee and Mason (2010) provided human capital investment and consumption rates data showing participation in human capital investment and consumption which tends to verify the reliability of the results of some studies that elderly standard of living are positively affected when there is simultaneous human capital investment.

Descriptive Analysis of the Demographic Data

Data were collected from using a 13 items survey questionnaire and the County census, revenue, schools' population documents. The survey questions centered and bounded within the County targeted population for the purpose of understanding the correlation between population decline and the effect on long-term economic growth. Participation of the survey was purposeful and voluntary. The participants may choose at their own volition to withdraw from participating in the survey. With 25 of the 50 participants completing and returning the survey, the response rate was attributed to 50%. However, of the 25 survey received, 21 were farmers and 4 non-farmers. Also, 15 participants were targeted for interview, 10 participated in the interview, 2 are Farmers and 8 were Non-Farmers. In all, the participants' rate for interview was 95%. The survey profile included sex (gender), age, and employment demography. Many other factors were also considered in the category. Among them were knowledge base implications of the targeted population. In this category, SPSS Guttman Scaling response was used for each of the coded responses that were analyzed. (See Table 1—shows the relationships between survey interview items and the research questions.)

In the survey, participants were asked, in some cases, to narrate their concerns, feelings, and degree of beliefs. The wide variety of participants demography between the Farming and Non-Farming communities ranges from 18-24 (n-1) = 5%; 25-34 (n-1) = 5%; 35-49 (n-12) = 45%; 50-64 (n-9) = 35%; over 65 (n-2) = 10%. The study compared the sample demographics of all participants as shown on Table 5.

Table 5

Survey Sample Response Rate

	Population overall	Participant responded
Participants	100%	50%
Males	54%	46%
Females	52%	48%
Farming	42%	58%
Non-farming	59%	41%
Highest category (ages 35-49)	58%	42%
Lowest category (ages 18-34)	97%	3%

In addition, 60% of the respondents chose sales tax as the principle source of revenues compared to 40% over all. 81% of participants responded that the population of the county is declining compared to 19% over all. 56% responded in ratio 7 out of a scale of 10 that the economy of Pierce County is growing compared to 44% over all who thought to the contrary. 42% observed and responded that (age 65+) have adequate standard of living compared to 58% over all that had a different view. The county per capita income was $14,055 as per the 2000 census figure. The unemployed rate is 4.1% compared to 3.2% State-wide.

Descriptive Analysis of the Independent Variables

The descriptive analyses of independent variables are stated in order of significance: emigration, mortality rate, fertility rate, elderly needs, and population decline. ANOVA, t test analysis, and simple linear regression analysis were used to analyze the farming and non-farming participating samples. The age group categories of 35-49 were considered to be the dominant determinant of participation. Older participants that are stakeholders in the various portfolios of investments are most likely to participate in surveys. However, higher elderly needs that tend to affect standard of living are a significant variable. There is most likely a close association between the age categories of 35-49 and 50-64 with elderly needs as shown in the response ratio. The variables between mortality and fertility rates as a result of the effect on population and economic growth are significant at the .05 level. However, there appears to be some relationship between all the variables as in regards to economic growth and the population stabilization processes. Maestas and Zissimopoulos (2010), Prettner and Prskawetz (2010), and Birchenall (2007) argued that investing in human capital affect lower fertility which prompt higher investments in education and correspondingly affect long-term higher per capita output that promulgate adequate standard of living for the elderly. Dasgupta (2007) argued that growth in gross domestic product (GDP) per capita is a significant benefit to adequate standard of living that also, encourages sustainable economic development.

Descriptive Analysis of the Dependent Variables

The descriptive analysis examined the following dependent variables: employment, education, human capital, technology, innovation, and economic growth. It should be noteworthy to state that education is a significant determinant in dependent variable whether is measured in degrees or years of schooling or training. Thus, as stated in Welty assertion (cited in Sertich, 2004) some of the critical components needed for rural regions to strive are: Education, Sense of Place, Investments, and Collaboration among leadership to formulate economic development.

Employment, human capital, innovation, and technology are other significant determinant variables to a sustainable long-term growth. The results of various analyses have shown a determined factor between the variables. Mollick (2006) supported the notion that innovation, advanced technology and education compliments each other as a determining factor that influences local economic growth that trigger to a higher concentration of broader economic activities around other demographical areas.

The Survey Results Initiatives

The researcher administered a 13-item survey of self-design, the PEGS, to 25 participants. Of these, 13 were women and 12 were men. Twenty-one identified their business as farming and 4 as non-farming. The age breakdown of respondents was as follows: 18-24 $(n = 1)$, 25-34 $(n = 1)$, 35-49 $(n = 12)$, 50-64 $(n = 9)$, over 65 $(n = 2)$.

Item 4 of the PEGS asked, "What types of tax data are used to define Pierce County's economic growth?" Eleven respondents checked sales tax, nine checked property tax, and five were not sure. The survey also asked if the county's population is declining. Nineteen said yes, five said no, and one was not sure. Participants who answered yes were invited to explain their answer. They cited the fact that the county is subject to overall census trends, the school-age population is declining, people need bigger farms to stay afloat, and family size is decreasing.

Asked whether elderly residents of Pierce County will have an adequate standard of living after retirement, 11 participants said yes, 5 said no, and 9 were not sure. The PEGS also asked respondents to describe whether the mortality and fertility rates in Pierce County are decreasing or increasing. Eleven said the mortality rate is increasing, 3 said it is decreasing, and 11 were not sure. Regarding the fertility rate, 2 thought it is increasing, 15 thought it is decreasing, and 8 were not sure.

Survey participants were also asked to rate the economic growth of Pierce County on a scale of 1 to 10. Their average ranking was 6, with a mode of 7 and a median of 6. Another survey item asked participants whether locating a college in Pierce County would be desirable. Fourteen respondents said yes, 7 said no, and 4 were not sure.

The Interview Results Initiatives

In addition to administering the PEGS to 25 respondents, the researcher interviewed 10 additional participants, using the same questions as a starting point. Like the survey participants, interviewees were chosen by purposive, non-proportional, criterion sampling based on their knowledge of the County. The semi-structured, face-to-face interviews were conducted at times and places convenient to participants. Interviews were guided, consistent, and comprehensive. Although the PEGS were used as the basis for interview questions, participants were encouraged to elaborate on their initial responses.

Because respondents were not comfortable being tape-recorded, I summarized their responses in writing. The primary purpose of the interviews was to elicit richer data by enabling participants to explain and elaborate their answers. Accordingly, the responses summarized in this section reflect those interview questions that prompted the greatest elaboration.

In discussing reasons for population decline in the US Northern County, interviewees pointed to the fact that economies of scale in a farming community dictate larger, more heavily mechanized farms, which means fewer people are involved in working the land. People who formerly might have been employed in farming move to larger towns and cities in search of knowledge-based careers. In talking about the postretirement prospects of elderly county residents, interviewees noted that most retirees continue to receive some residual income from their agricultural property. Some have pensions, all are eligible for Social Security, and many have maintained a long-term commitment to savings and investments. Respondents tended to think that the County offers adequate social services for its elderly residents. On the negative side, interviewees pointed to the rising costs of health care.

In discussing economic growth in the US Northern County, interviewees emphasized the importance of attracting manufacturing jobs to the county and reeducating the labor force, especially through technical education. They were divided on the advisability of locating a 2-year technical college in the county. Supporters argued that in an agriculturally based area, most of the potential labor force would benefit from the training offered at a technical college. Detractors pointed to the fact that neighboring counties have similar educational institutions and questioned whether an additional facility in the area would be viable.

The Results of the Statistical Data Analysis

The aim of the simple regression model was to achieve confidence in the results of survey and interview responses. According to Creswell (2007), comparative analyses strengthen the validity of results; as such, the statistical test used in this study was the
t test. This statistical test established the presence or absence of the linear correlation between population decline (independent variable) and its effect on economic growth (dependent variable). The *t* test was used to explain the variables that were important in determining the multicollinearity of the data. SPSS open code and qualitative frequencies were used to analyze the reliability of respondents' responses. Huberman and Wiles (1994) supported the use of general data analysis strategies that make contrasts and comparisons, highlight and identify codes, and determine frequencies that are commonly used in qualitative research analysis.

The *t* test statistic was used to test for the correlation of the independent and dependent variables (population declining and economic growth). The calculation was based on Aczel and Sounderpandian's (2006) equation:

$$t = \frac{(X_1 - X_2) - (\mu_1 - \mu_2)_0}{\sqrt{S_{2/p}(1/n_1 + 1/n_2)}}$$

The *t* test correlations used a two-tailed test ($H_0: \mu_1 - \mu_2 = 0$ versus $H_1: \mu_1 - \mu_2 \neq 0$), which indicated a distribution of 22 degrees of freedom (*df*) and a result of -6.244, which is within the rejection region at a significant level (α) of 5%. Since the *p* value of 0.1277 is less than 5%, it can be concluded with confidence that the difference in population $1 - \alpha$ (95%) resulted in $-10 \pm 3.32251 = \{13.323, -6.677\}$ based on school population sample data and the county revenues, leading to the overall conclusion that there is no correlation between population decline and economic growth in the County.

Because the t tests revealed a disparity due to multicollinearity of the data, regression and ANOVA analyses were conducted to solve for collinearity. Results of this analysis confirmed that there was no correlation between population decline and economic growth.

A one-sample Kolmogorov-Smirnov N-par test was used to analyze three items on the PEGS: population decline, elderly standard of living after retirement, and economic growth. The results of this test confirmed that the County population is declining and that respondents have enough evidence that economic growth of the County is increasing and that most of the retired elderly population will have an adequate standard of living after retirement.

An analysis of gender and elderly adequate standard of living after retirement showed a correlation of .03 on a 95% confidence interval (CI) of the difference between lower (-.80) and upper (-.12) on a t test of -2.75. Pair three, age and economic growth, showed a correlation of $-.13$ on a 95% CI of the difference between lower (1.02) and upper (2.22) on a t test of 5.48. The standard error mean was controlled (below .3) at the same 95% CI. Differences among the three items (Q5, Q7, Q12) are shown in Table 6.

Table 6

ANOVA: Economic Growth and Population Decline

Source	Type III Sum of Squares	Df	Mean Square
Corrected Model	38.883	14	2.777
Intercept	458.759	1	458.759
Q7	1.646	2	.823
Q5	5.333	2	2.667
Q12	21.524	3	7.175
Q7 * Q5	2.012	1	2.012
Q7 * Q12	5.427	4	1.357
Q5 * Q12	2.036	1	2.036
Q7 * Q5 * Q12	.000	0	
Error	49.422	21	2.353
Total	1233.000	36	
Corrected Total	88.306	35	

The Qualitative Coding Results

To identify any trends or patterns in interview data, the researcher used the manual technique of theme identification. This process actually began during the interview itself as the researcher reviewed participants' answers with them and asked additional probing questions, if necessary, to elicit richer detail. In recording these responses by hand, the researcher began to get a glimpse of themes and patterns in the data. Huberman and Wiles (1994) supported the general data analysis process of identifying codes and frequencies of use as an indispensible method used in qualitative analysis.

Qualitative coding is a procedure to organize data into systematic categories. Qualitative coding lends clarity and pragmatism to coded items. Appendix F displays the coding information the researcher used. Coded themes represent items that surfaced during data analysis. Each item represents respondents' opinions or viewpoints. Each item in the category was formulated with code numbers that represent participants' responses to questions. The symbol n demonstrates the frequency with which participants responded to a particular category of items. Participants' responses are summarized below:

1. Are you male or female?
   Participants were evenly divided (50% each) based on gender.
2. Are you in the farming or non-farming business?
   The farming business accounted for 58% of respondents, compared to 41% for non-farming business.
3. Are you between the ages of . . . ?
   The highest percentage of participants (42%) fell in the 35-49 categories, and the lowest percentage (3%) was in the 18-34 categories.
4. What type of tax data are used to determine Pierce County's economic growth?
   The majority of respondents (60%) chose sales tax as the principal source of revenue in Pierce County. Figure 1 shows detailed result.
5. Is the population of Pierce County declining?
   Most participants (81%) said the population is declining. Among the reasons they listed for decline were that Pierce

County is an agricultural county, economies of scale for farmers, and migration of residents to bigger towns and cities in search of knowledge-based careers.

6. Will the elderly (age 68 +) in Pierce County have an adequate standard of living after retirement?

    Forty-two percent of participants responded affirmatively to this question, compared to 39% who were not sure. Respondents noted that most retirees received residual income from their agricultural land after retirement; others receive pensions and Social Security benefits. Participants noted that high health care costs might affect the living standard of elderly county residents. They thought that Pierce County offers adequate social services for the elderly. Participants speculated that most of the elderly population is financially stable due to their long-term commitment to savings and investments.

7. On a scale of 1-10, 10 being the highest score, please, identify the rate of the economic growth of Pierce County.

    A majority of respondents (56%) rated Pierce County's economic growth as 7. They said that attracting manufacturing jobs to the county and reeducating the labor force (farmers and high school graduates) through technical education will contribute to stable economic growth.

8. Is opening a 2-year vocational technical college a desirable concept for the county in the future?

Half of the participants responded affirmatively to this question, and 31% rejected the idea of a 2-year college. Those who favored a 2-year technical college said that in a mechanized farming community, most of the labor force would benefit from the training provided by such an institution. Those opposed to the idea said that a technical college would not be viable in the county due to costs and the fact that neighboring counties already have 2-year colleges.

Figure 1 shows economic growth in Pierce County by age. The primary reason for changing population dynamics is the aging of baby boomers (residents between the ages of 35 and 65) and the emigration of younger adults (ages 18 to 34). The county's median age still remains below 34. As the county's population ages, there may be serious long-term implications for the economy, raising the question, "Will Pierce County have a sufficient labor force and an adequate standard of living for its residents"? As observed, migration to the county has remained insignificant while fertility has slightly increased since the mid 2000s, resulting in a 0.5% increase in the school population between 2007 and 2008. This increase resulted in a 0.1% growth in revenue, as shown in Tables 3 and 4. Most surrounding counties within 50 miles have a growing school-age population as a result of young families being attracted to more robust communities with colleges and college graduates—an extension of human capital resources for those counties.

According to Kinghorn and Justis (2008), to plan for a sustained growth and development, counties must increase their school-age population, which in turn increases the number of young adults. They also argued that migration influenced by the socioeconomic environment attract new residents to a community, which affects population change and thereby improves economic prospects and quality of life.

Henderson and Akers (2009) supported Kinghorn and Justis's (2008) notion that rural counties face the challenge of aging populations.

> Aging populations are expected to slow economic growth, and rural migration patterns are both accelerating and mitigating this trend. In recent years, many rural residents have left their counties after graduation from high school in search of job opportunities. (Henderson & Akers, 2009, p. 105).

Henderson and Akers (2009) noted the return of middle-aged adults in their 30s to some rural counties and that "middle-aged in-migrants are fewer than out-migrating young adults, which tends to offset some population losses in some rural counties, even smaller, farm-dependent communities" (pp. 107-108). They further stated that although the out-migration of young adults remains worrisome, losses have diminished over the past decade and the exodus of young adults has led to aging populations in small rural counties.

Lee and Mason (2010) cited conventional theory to suggest that as income increases, fertility decreases and human capital investments rise, due to the quantity and quality of economic interaction. They argued that low fertility and an aging population may not have anticipated adverse affects on standards of living because planned population aging is consistent with bringing a highly educated population and a comfortable standard of living to a community.

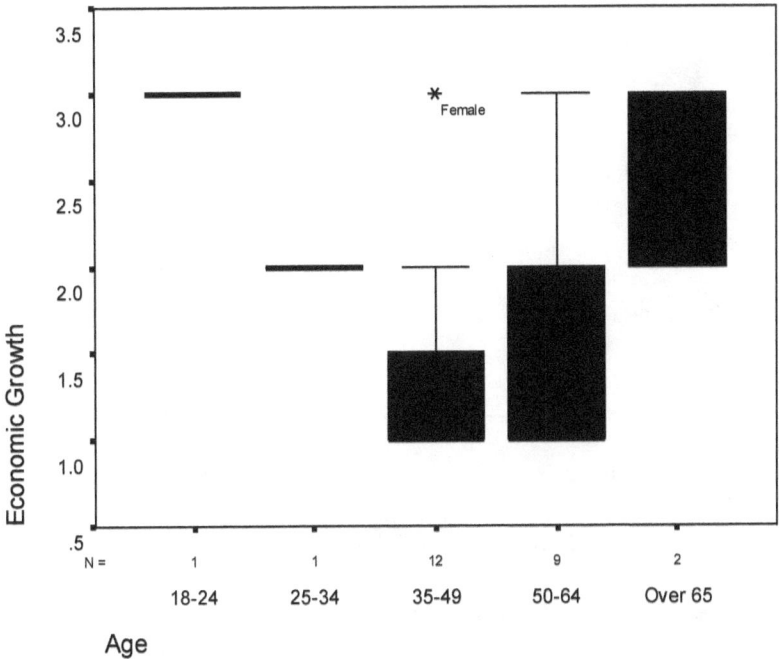

Figure 1. Economic growth stem-leaf plot.

The Quantitative Results

The scatter plot in Figure 2 illustrates the regression equation y = 1.493x + 274.5, and the regression line indicates that Y is uncorrelated with X. As such, Y may be either large or small where X is large, and vice versa, indicating that there is no systematic trend in Y as X increases. The slope of the line $ß_1$ is equal to zero. According to Aczel and Sounderpandian (2006), "The most important statistical tests in simple linear regression is the test of whether the slope parameter $ß_1$ is equal to zero" (p. 535). Since $ß_1$ is zero, it can be concluded that there is no correlation between decline in population and economic growth in Pierce County. In other words,

$$H_0 : ß_1 = 0$$
$$H_1 : ß_1 = 0$$

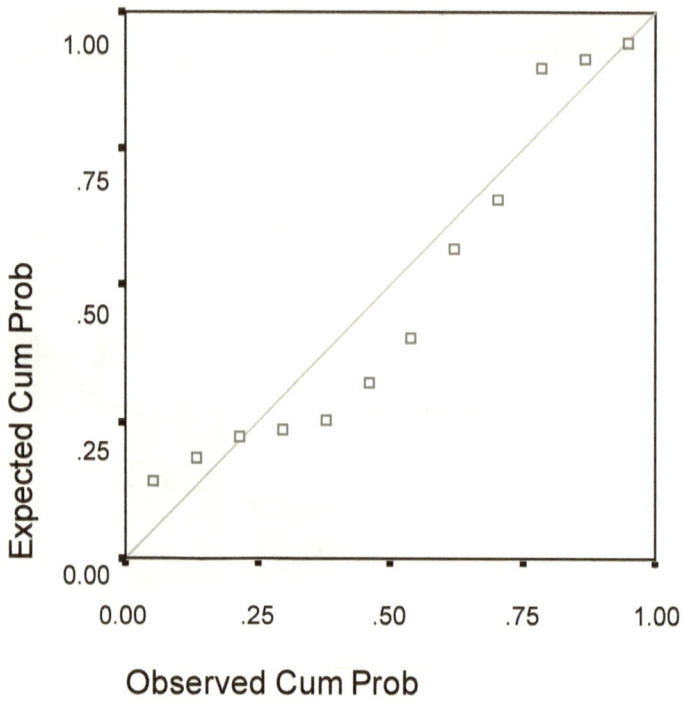

Figure 2. Simple linear regression slope.

The two-tailed *t* test indicates that the regression slope, if it equals zero, shows that the two variables have no linear relationship. Conversely, if the slope does not equal zero, the two variables have a linear relationship. The test used to determine rejection and non-rejection of the null hypothesis is as follows:

$$t^{(n-2)} = b_1 - (\beta_1)_0 / s(b_1)$$

This formula calculates Estimate — Hypothesized parameter value / Standard error of estimator. The hypothesis test indicates that because the critical point of α is 0.05, with ± 1.98, and the *t* distribution is 0.84154, there is no evidence of a linear relationship between population decline and economic growth in the County. Aczel and Sounderpandian (2006) noted that the most frequent use of regression analysis is to show predictions that are not perfect and are subject to error attributed to "uncertainty in estimation as well as the natural variation of points about the regression line" (pp. 552–553).

Summary

Sample selection was purposeful and judgmental because participants were selected based on their knowledge of the County. Semi-structured interviews were conducted at respondents' convenience. The interview strategy was based on resource knowledge of core groups. Creswell (2007) noted that this type of interview approach enhances reliability of the findings. A Population and Economic Growth Survey coding scheme of 13 items was used to gather and analyze data. The mixed-methods approach facilitated the formulation and interpretation of results. According to Creswell (2007), qualitative and qualitative data can be gathered at the same time. Some quantitative data were obtained from public domain and official records; qualitative data were from individual interviews and surveys.

Statistical analysis was based on a simple regression t test, which aimed to achieve confidence in responses from the survey and interviews. Creswell (2007) noted that comparative analyses strengthen validity. The statistical t test used for both qualitative and quantitative data calculations established the lack of linear correlation between independent and dependent variables.

CHAPTER 5

Population Stabilization and Long-Term Economic Growth Model for Sparsely Populated Counties

One of the goals of this study was to formulate a population stabilization and long-term economic growth model for sparsely populated counties that will help support possible policy changes. This chapter consists of an interpretation of the major findings in relation to the research questions, a discussion of the population and economic stabilization model for social change, and recommendations for action and for further research.

Interpretation of Findings Based on Research Questions

Research Question 1

The researcher observed the dwindling of the prospective regional demographic distribution in the local manpower of the US Northern County in ND. According to the U.S Census figures, over the past 20 years based on the age groupings of men and women between 18 to 29 years, the manpower growth have been in decline despite the county rapidly growing economy. In the same token, however, the largest shares of growth to the economy have been attributed to the aging population between the ages of 65 years and above. In other words, over the next two decades, if the status-quo remain the same, the aging population will be reserved the burden of generating nearly half the growth in the local working-age population of the county. Eberstadt (2010) asserted that the prospects of shrinking manpower are deterrent to economic growth especially when broken down into subsidiary age-group components. He indicated that younger workers are important for economic growth, because they typically have higher levels of education and better knowledge of the latest technology. Thus, in the US Northern County of North Dakota over the past 20 years, growth in this pool of young manpower has undergone a severe deceleration due to immigrating to urban cities in search of jobs and higher education.

Malthus (1796) predicted that growth of an economy can be measured by the stability of the population. Duesterberg (2007) and Mollick (2006) proposed that growth in skilled workers plus productivity contributes to a propensity for economic growth. Smith (1776) asserted that productivity capacity, along with the affluence of skilled workers, regulates long-term growth and the capacity of increasing wealth. These predictions were not realized in the County, where the economy has progressed despite a steady decline in population.

A one-sample Kolmogorov-Smirnov N-par test was used to analyze three variables: population decline, economic growth, and elderly standard of living after retirement. Results suggested that the respondents have enough evidence for their assessment that the County population is declining, the economy is growing, and that most of the elderly population will have an adequate standard of living after retirement.

Gender differences and standard of living after retirement showed a correlation of .03 on a 95% confidence interval (CI) of the difference between lower (-.80) and upper (-.12) on a t test of -2.75. Age differences and economic growth showed a correlation of -.13 on a 95% confidence interval (CI) of the difference between lower (1.02) and upper (2.22) on a t test of 5.48. In the pair analysis, the standard error mean was controlled below .3 on a 95% CI. This result portrays the County inclining towards a long-term economic growth. Overall, the results indicated that respondents were knowledgeable about the community.

Quantitative analysis results showed that the simple linear regression t test depicted a slope of the line β_1 equal to zero. Aczel and Sounderpandian (2006) indicated that the most important statistical test in simple linear regression is whether the slope parameter β_1 is equal to zero. As such, results of this study suggest that there is no linear relationship between the variables population decline and economic growth. Two-tailed test results showed that the true regression slope is equal to zero, which is an indicator that the two variables (population decline and economic growth) have no linear relationship and do not correlate. The t distribution test result indicated that the t ratio compared with the critical points of $p = 0.05$ and n - 2 degree of freedom (df) with ± 1.98, and a t distribution of 0.84154. Since the t distribution 0.84154 < 1.98, there is no evidence of a linear relationship between population decline and economic growth in County.

Research Questions 2 and 3

These two questions addressed emigration and its effect on long-term economic growth. Combining these questions helps explain emigration as a source of brain drain in a rural population for the benefit of urban development. Lucas's (1988) empirical and theoretical model predicts a relationship between education and employment in affecting emigration. Lucas's linear regression test results on the effect of education on economic growth showed a linear relationship between the two.

The first stage of Lucas's (1988) test involves calculating the average duration of training the working population, or the average school attendance rate, to show the level of long-term human capital. Several approximations are proposed in Lucas's test pattern: illiteracy rates, level of schooling or number of diplomas when one leaves the educational system, and average annual wages. The second stage of Lucas's tests involves measuring human capital in relation to training (education). To verify the results, a supplementary estimate was proposed based on annual average wages and their relationship to human capital. Lucas asserted that there is a negative relationship between the growth rate of human capital and the average length of training. Lucas's model is essentially normative rather than predictive because it could not develop a self-sustained economic theory with variables necessary to sustain economic growth.

Azariadis and Drazen (1990) argued that training duration and the stock of human capital change the relationship between the dependent variable and explanatory variables. They asserted that the coefficient of correlation is important in introducing a new variable that improves Lucas's (1988) model. Lucas supported the endogenous theorists' assertion that economic growth is a function of human capital stock and does not improve efficiency of the labor force (employment) without the necessary knowledge base (education). Mollick (2006), Chen (2006), and Dasgupta (2007) argued that technological expansion, skilled migration, political and education influences regional and local economic growth. They confirmed human capital as an essential factor in economic growth. Mollick concluded that emigration causes a reduction in skilled labor, which results in brain drain in the affected communities and depresses long-term economic growth. Mollick did not conclusively determine whether education is the main engine of economic growth, but he proposed further study of that potential relationship.

Bucci and Torre (2009) study on population and economic growth with human physical capital investment concluded in their findings that physical capital and formal education has to complement each other because increase in supply of physical capital will spur demand and eventually produce new human capital that will attract long-term growth potential. Qureshi (2009) supported Bucci and Torre (2009) argument and asserted that human capital investment is an essential economic factor to economic indicator. He argued that even though resources maybe diverted by policy makers to other factor in the economy that may stimulate economic growth, he warned that priority on higher public expenditures has to be applied to human capital. He proposed that not only does human capital investment improve human development indicator, it also, supplement substantial economic growth in the long-run.

The qualitative and quantitative results of this study provided contextual insights on education, employment, elderly retirees, emigration, and economic growth. The most notable data were interview responses, which were clearly presented and revealed an honest representation of participants' feelings and thoughts. Interview questions were designed to encourage the free flow of conversation. Creswell (2007) stated that a well-designed interview should be crafted with the most useful information to answer the research questions. Bailey (1978) asserted that interview process is useful to probe for more specific answers and noted that questions can be repeated for clarity. This case study employed interview questions that were consistent with Hammersley and Atkinson's (1995) interview protocol.

Thematic categories were developed during the qualitative coding process, as discussed in the previous chapter. Each category was assigned a number. At the end of the coding process, the collective anecdotal results were transcribed into separate and mutually exclusive thematic segments. Turnover was recognized in examining those thematic segments with highest frequencies. The following thematic segments were identified:

> Farming *(n = 21)* with a marginal percentage response of 84%.
> Non-farming *(n = 4)* with a marginal percentage response of 16%.
> Five themes were based on age group: 18-24, 25-34, 35-49, 50-64, and 65+. The results were as follows:

> 18-24 *(n =1)* with a marginal percentage response of 4%.
> 25-34 *(n = 1)* with a marginal percentage response of 4%.
> 35-49 *(n = 12)* with a marginal percentage response of 48%.
> 50-64 *(n = 9)* with a marginal percentage response of 36%.
> Over 65 *(n = 2)* with a marginal percentage response of 8%.

Participants were asked whether they would favor establishing a 2-year technical vocational college in the county. Two-third of them responded favorably, and a third rejected the idea. Those not in favors of adding an institution of higher education in the area argued that the county's small population would not be able to support a college. They also noted that neighboring counties already have colleges. Those participants who responded positively to the idea of a 2-year vocational technical college argued that it would encourage the retention of a skilled labor force and encourage healthy human capital that would strengthen long-term economic growth in the county.

Participants in the farming business were most highly represented in the age categories 35-49 ($n = 12$, 48%) and 50-64 ($n = 9$, 36%). The majority of respondents in the farming business supported the idea of education through training and retraining the labor force as an engine of long-term economic growth. This conviction is consistent with the ideas of economic historians such as North and Thomas (1973) and Landes (1998), who argued that advanced societies are wealthy because educational institutions have enabled the populace to improve their knowledge of the newest available technology, which provides innovation and growth in their communities. Also relevant is the assertion by Clark et al. (2010) that when labor force participation stays constant, the labor force will reflect an older and smaller population. If the labor force rate of decline exceeds the rate of population decline, there are profound implications for the rate of economic growth.

Zhuang and St. Juliana (2010) argued that even though a population increase can contribute to economic growth, an excessive increase can slow economic growth. They postulated that innovation through research and development will lead to faster growth, noting that the impact of such R&D may depend on whether a sufficient technological capacity is available in the economy. Zhuang and St. Juliana support the idea of investing in education as a way to increase an economy's capacity to accommodate innovation and thereby contribute to long-term economic growth and development.

Research Question 4

When asked whether they thought elderly county residents would have an adequate standard of living after retirement, 42% of participants responded affirmatively, and 39% were are not sure. Respondents noted that many retirees have income from their rented agricultural land. Some receive pensions and Social Security benefits. One threat to financial security is the high cost of health care. One half of the participants thought that the County offers adequate social services for its elderly population. They also said that most elderly residents are financially stable due to their long-term in savings and investments.

Zhang (2004) argued that Social Security benefits stimulate GNP growth and increase investment in human capital without having an effect on savings. His results were based on a two-sector growth model, which derived data from bequests, savings, education, and fertility. Zhang posited that an aging population can be a dynamic force that will enhance human capital investment and economic growth. Prettner and Prskawetz (2010) and Gruescu (2007) assertions on how exogenous growth models was used to explain the linkage between economic growth and population size, human capital accumulation, and the capital intensity of the workers. They argued that changes in the decomposition of the workforce and an increase in population size will affect aggregate productivity that can boost capital in the population. Bloom and Sousa-Poza (2010) also argued that declining population on an aging population will affect economic growth and lower standard of living. They asserted that the effect of population declining in size can be an impediment to economic growth and capital dilution in the population. Bucci (2008), on the other hand, argued that technology, human capital accumulation, and R&D activities are substantial source of endogenous technological progress that can stimulate long-term economic growth.

Yakita (2006) noted that longevity in a developing economy is due to a decline in the adult mortality rate. Yakita asserted that increased longevity and adequate education encourage savings and capital investment, which translate into economic growth. Yakita also predicted that the effect of capital spillovers would remain strong as mortality declines, and that lower inflation would prevail as growth increases. Yakita concluded that economic growth does not affect population. This point is critical in regard to the present study because it helps inform a theory that would benefit rural counties and serve as a basis for further research.

Prettner and Prskawetz (2010) argued that extended low fertility rates will lead to lower population growth, which will decrease population size and subsequently cause a decline in GDP and potentially increase the wage distribution inequality between age groups. Lee and Mason (2010), on the other hand, argued that "low fertility and slower population growth will lead to increased capital intensity and higher per capita income" (pp. 159-160), which affects savings and labor force growth rates. The assumption is that higher per capita income is generally synonymous with exponential growth, which may eventually affect wage distribution in the labor force.

Construction of Population Stabilization and Economic Growth Model

One of the researcher's goals in this study was to develop a population stabilization and economic growth model. The theory is based on the work of Lucas (1988), and its development follows five steps.

Step 1: *Determine Effect of Development on Economic Growth*

Development in rural communities depends on steady growth initiatives. An effective development plan will focus on long-term economic growth. Public policies must complement governmental initiatives. The components needed for a rural initiative include the following:

1. Pride of community and involvement in higher education.
2. A governing body embedded with entrepreneurial spirit.
3. Cooperation and collaboration with other rural and regional leaders.
4. Investment in research, innovation, and infrastructure.
5. Education and skills retraining.

For rural communities such as the US Northern County, to maintain long-term economic growth, policymakers should encourage savings and investment and emphasize on educational system that produces human capital and skilled labor needed in advanced agro-based technologies and machineries. The prime objective is to focus on population stabilization by reducing the emigration of skilled labor to urban counties and maintaining long-term economic growth in the process.

Step 2: *Develop Policies to Stabilize Population Decline*

Governments in rural communities should be concerned about the rapid emigration of their populace and should develop policies that will assist in stabilizing population and promote long-term economic growth. Azariadis and Drazen (1990) supported Lucas's (1988) population model, which the present study replicates. Human capital investment, an engine to the economic development in the County, is mostly dependent on elderly retirees. Based on quantitative findings, this study showed that population decline does not correlate with economic growth, which depends on education, technology, savings, and investment. Azariadis and Drazen and Lucas concluded that population stabilization contributes to long-term economic growth in conjunction with human capital investment, education, advanced technologies, and innovation. These components suggest broad guidelines appropriate for developing a population stabilization and economic model.

Step 3: *Promote High Standard of Living and Economic Growth among Elderly*

The PEGS results suggest that the standard of living among retired residents of Pierce County will improve steadily as economic growth remains strong. Retirees represent the majority of investors in Pierce County. Dasgupta (2007) asserted that economic growth through human capital investment promotes a better quality of life. He argued that growth is measured in real GDP per capita, which is compatible with sustainable economic development. Tonnessen (2008) supported Dasgupta's conclusion that counties should stabilize population and provide incentives that encourage long-term economic growth.

Dasgupta (2007) argued that education advances in science and technology, and reinvestment in development are essential factors for long-term economic growth. Duesterberg (2007) argued that long-term economic growth potential is related to population stability. He emphasized the importance of mechanized agriculture and manufacturing industries, which contribute to economic growth through employment and taxes. Mitchell and Mosler (2006) posited that long-term growth depends on the quantity of capital investment. They noted that adequate savings and investments by most elderly residents represent a form of capital that helps and grow economy. Tonnessen (2008) and Mitchell and Mosler (2006) asserted that environmental sustainability is important for economic growth. Mitchell and Mosler supported their assertions and also stated that enlightened environmental policies are necessary to encourage capital investment in local economies.

Step 4: *Foster Employment and Economic Growth*

A sustainable employment plan that promotes long-term economic growth in local communities should have the following characteristics:

1. Community involvement in education (e.g., technical vocational institution).
2. A governing body with entrepreneurial spirit.
3. Cooperation and collaboration with other rural and regional community leaders in knowledge sharing.

4. Investment in research.
5. Encouragement of savings and investments.
6. Encouragement of creativity and innovation.
7. Teamwork that promotes growth outside traditional vocational roles.
8. A flexible business cycle.
9. Optimum environment for technological capabilities and advantages.

The goal of a sustainable employment plan is to reduce involuntary unemployment to zero. Thus, Smith (1776) and Malthus's (1796) contextual frameworks are vital in understanding the influence of employment and stabilizing population on long-term economic growth that is crucial in the formation of the model.

Step 5: *Recognize Influence of Technology and Innovation*

Local authorities should explore technological and innovative capabilities in their communities. Political leaders should use their influence through polity to encourage technological initiatives in their communities. Mencken, Bader, and Polson (2006) argued that such action can be accomplished through civic engagement, the results of which are vital to a community's socioeconomic well-being. Mollick (2006) emphasized technological expansion, skilled labor development, and education. He stated that strengthened governmental policies will foster greater economic growth than can be achieved solely through a concentration of economic activity. Such policy development requires strong political leadership.

Social Change Implications

According to Dasgupta (2007), growth in real GDP per capita is simultaneous with quality of life and is compatible with sustainable economic development. He argued that an investment in education, science, and technology represents a bequest to future generations and enhances their ability to achieve economic prosperity. Mencken, Bader, and Polson (2006) emphasized the importance of civic engagement by policy makers in creating the socioeconomic conditions that are crucial to growth. They also called for further study of the association between economic growth and civic engagement. Lyson and Tolbert (2003) asserted that with net sales from traditional markets, competitive civil engagement boosts growth. Lobao and Hooks (2003) noted that another component of growth is political elites who influence government-subsidized contracts (e.g., defense contracts, military bases, government infrastructure).

Blanchard and Matthew (2006) argued that communities should be cautious with regards to multinational corporate influences in local community decision making because of the potential to undermine civic engagement and affect long-term growth. Mollick (2006) asserted that technological expansion, skilled workforce development, and education can influence regional and local economic growth. He argued that economic growth can be achieved with a concentration of economic activities. Mollick noted that investment and income from wages help stabilize population and foster economic growth. He stated the need for further research on population and economic growth. As with many constructs associated with population and economic growth, socioeconomic theory is employed as a way of sharing theoretical ideas with other scholars. An essential discipline is sociology, which considers social relationships and behavior. The sociological perspective challenges familiar surroundings in order to critically assess a community of people. Mollick (2006) noted that another important factor in sociological analysis is technology, which is one way a community promotes economic growth.

To sustain long-term economic development in the US Northern County, the researcher required stabilization in emigration from the county. Social change is necessary to revitalize manufacturing industries and increase agricultural and human capital investment. According to Gruescu (2007), investments in education positively affect economic growth, a conclusion that is reinforced by the results of the present study. Investment in technical education in an agricultural region can be associated with long-term economic growth and improved quality of life.

Recommendations for Sustainable Growth In A Declining Population

Based on the results of this study, several action steps can be recommended:

1. It is important to recognize education as a quality of life issue. Technical vocational educational training can help reduce the rate of emigration, especially among young adults. Vocational education provides a source of training and retraining in new technologies, enhances labor skills, improves the motivational spirit of the populace, and promotes long-term growth and stable migration.
2. Technology and innovation are important components of economic planning and community development. Endogenous growth theorists support education and technological change through innovation as factors that will promote economic growth. Investment in education encourages advances in science and technology and fosters long-term sustainable growth and development. Local authorities who want to stabilize population in their counties should encourage innovation while also minimizing pressure on the environment.
3. Human capital investment is an engine of economic development. Dasgupta (2007) asserted that economic growth through human capital investment is heavily dependent on savings and investments by the elderly. Adequate savings and investments as practiced by the elderly in a local community contribute to economic growth and improved quality of life.
4. Bloom and Sousa-Poza (2010) proposed a declining population on an aging population will affect economic growth, capital dilution, and lower standard of living in the entire size of the population. Bucci (2008), on the other hand, argued that technology, human capital accumulation/investment, and R&D activities are substantial source of endogenous technological progress that can stimulate long-term economic growth.

Local authorities should promote investment in technological and innovative capabilities in their communities. Political leaders should use their influence through polity to encourage technological initiatives.

Policy makers should encourage civic engagement among citizens. These actions will serve as another platform for local authorities to stabilize declining populations and foster long-term economic growth through technological advancement, skilled labor development, and technical education.

Although, the research document in this study did not totally support a correlation between population decline and economic growth. Survey and interview participants, on the other hand, overwhelmingly asserted that a decline in population may affect long-term economic growth. Based on these findings, it is recommended that further studies be conducted that take advantage of new census data as they become available following the 2010 census. Future research should also include qualitative studies that reflect people's attitudes and impressions, the collapse of once-vibrant townships, the economic effects of emigration from rural to urban areas, and the effect of fertility and mortality rates on a local economy.

The Researcher's Personal Reflections

It has been a remarkable experience to plan, organize, and implement the data collection involved in this challenging and enriching case study. The self-designed survey was geared towards the needs, aspirations, and experiences of the targeted population. The study enables a selected few to speak for many in the communities that represent a US Northern County in North Dakota. Avoiding personal bias was a continuing challenge because the community the researcher studied was one in which he previously lived.

Summary

The researcher stated three implications that were viable for writing this text. First, the importance of recognizing education as a quality of life issue; for example, the availability and the provision of technical vocational educational training in rural counties can assist in stabilizing population and promote long-term economic growth. Second, technological innovation should be promoted, but not at the expense of environmental degradation. Third, elderly residents should be viewed, not as a drain on the economy, but as a source of population and economic stability.

GLOSSARY

Aging population: Residents of a particular community age 65 and older who are considered retired from the labor force.

Civil engagement: Policy making designed to attract government investment in a community.

Completion rate: The rate at which a given population or sample completes formal education. A high completion rate indicates a highly educated workforce.

Correlating coefficient: A statistical measure that indicates the direction of a relationship positive or negative, but ignoring signs that indicate the strength of associations. (Singleton & Straits, 2005, p. 55).

Countercyclical: A measurement that goes up with economic depression or contractions and down with economic expansion.

Economic growth: Revenue collected from properties, sales, and taxes and reinvested in service and agricultural industries.

Emigration: The voluntary movement of people from one geographic region to another.

Enterprise: A firm or a business organization consisting of different organizational structures.

Farming communities: Places where residents are predominantly involved in commercial and mechanized farming.

Gross domestic product (GDP): A measure of economic productivity that reflects goods and services, imports and exports, for a particular unit of analysis over a specified period.

Group population: For the purpose of this study, group population is defined as the total population count at a given period of time in Pierce County, North Dakota.

Human capital: People who are in the labor force or who are potential members of the labor force.

Human capital depreciation: A decline in the actual or potential labor force. Human capital depreciation can result from declining population (either a lower birth rate or higher emigration) and from the loss of applicable skills (by emigration or by an undereducated work force) in a particular population.

Intergenerational solidarity: A group of people of diverse ages who have unified community goals.

Job training: Learning by doing.

Market institutions: Financial facilities that facilitate saving, investments, and other monetary transactions in a community.

Nonfarming communities: Areas within the city limits of an incorporated town or city.

Operational: Describes "a research that would specify a value or category of a variable on each case" (Singleton & Straits, 2005, p. 78).

Population decline: A reduction in population size at a given place and time. Population decline is one of this study's independent variables.

Procyclical: A measurement that goes up with economic expansion and down with economic contraction.

Sampling procedure: The part of a research plan that indicates how cases are to be selected for observation (Singleton & Straits, 2005, p. 118).

Small county demography: Rural counties with population densities that are much lower than those of urban counties.

Sociology: The influences and the relationships of people and behavior, and their functionality.

Sociological perspective: A research perspective based on the assumption that a consideration of people's physical and social environmental aids in understanding a particular group of people.

Statistical significance: When associations between two variables are considered meaningful.

Theoretical framework: Theories used in an analytical formation for a case study.

REFERENCES

Aczel, A. D., & Sounderpandian, J. (2006). *Complete business statistics* (6th ed.). New York, NY: McGraw-Hill Irwin.

Aghion, P., & Howitt, P. (2005). "Growth with quality improving innovations: An integrated framework," in P. Aghion & S. Durlau (Eds.), *Handbook of economic growth* (pp. X-X), Amsterdam: North Holland.

Asmussen, K. J., & Creswell, J. W. (1995). Campus response to a student gunman. *Journal of Higher Education, 66*, 575-591.

Atoh, M. (2006). The current state of the world population: North-south contrast. *Asia Pacific Review, 7*(2), 121-135.

Autor, D., & Dorn, D. (2009). The job is getting old: Measuring changes in job opportunities using occupational age structure. *American Economic Review, 99*(2), 45-51.

Azarnert, L. V. (2006). Child mortality, fertility, and human capital accumulation. *Journal of Population Economics, 29*, 285-297.

Babbie, E. (2007). *Research methods for social work* (6th ed.) Belmont, CA: Thompson.

Bailey, K. D. (2007). *Methods of social research*. London, UK: Collier-Macmillan.

Baldwin, R. E., & Martin, P. (2004). Agglomeration and regional growth in handbook of regional and urban economics (4th ed.) J.V. Henderson & J.F. Thisse (Eds.) Amsterdam, Elsevier.

Benz, K. (2006). Saving Old McDonald's farm after South Dakota Farm Bureau, Inc. v. Hazeltine: Rethinking the role of the state, farming operations, the dominant commerce clause and growth management statues. *Natural Resources Journal, 46*(3), 793-830.

Bezruchka, S. (2009). The effect of economic recession on population health. *CMAJ Analysis*, 18.

Binder, D. A.(1992). Fitting Cox's proportional hazards models from survey data. *Biometrika, 79*, 139-147.

Birchenall, J. A. (2007). Escaping high mortality. *Journal of Economic Growth, 12*, 351-387.

Blanchard, T., & Matthew, T. L. (2006). The configuration of local economic power and civic participation in the global economy. *Social Forces, 84*(4), 224.

Bloom, D. E., & Sousa-Poza, A. (2010). Introduction to Special Issue of the European Journal of Population: Economic Consequences of Low Fertility in Europe. European Journal of Population Dordrecht. 26(2), 127.

Bloom, D. E., Canning, D., & Sevilla, J. (2003). The demographic dividend: A new perspective on the economic consequences of population change. Santa Monica, CA: Rand.

Broda, C., & Weinstein, D. (2006). Globalization and the gains from variety. *Quarterly Journal of Economics, 121*, 541-585.

Brown, D. C. (2005). Why ask why: Patterns and themes of causal attribution in the workplace. *Journal for Industrial Teachers Education, 33*(4), 47-65.

Chen, H. (2006). International migration and economic growth: A source country perspective. *Journal of Population Economics, 19*, 725-748.

City data. (2010). Pierce County, North Dakota. Retrieved July 8, 2010, from http://www.city-data.com/county/Pierce_County-ND.html

Clark, R. L., Ogawa, N., Kondo, M., & Matsukura, R. (2010). Population decline, labor force stability and the future of the Japanese economy. *European Journal of Population, 26*, 207-227.

Coleman, D. (2008). The demographic efforts of international migration in Europe. *Oxford Review of Economic Policy, 24*(3), 453-477.

Creswell, J. W. (2007). *Qualitative inquiry and research design: Choosing among five approaches*. Thousand Oaks, CA: Sage.

Dasgupta, P. (2007). Nature and the economy. *Journal of Applied Ecology, 44*, 475-487.

Duesterberg, T. J. (2007). When it comes to the economy, population matters. *The Competitive Edge, 13*, 1.

Eisner, E. W. (2005). *The enlightened eye: Qualitative inquiry and the enhancement of educational practice*. New York, NY: Macmillan.

Gilbert, N. (2001). *Social research update.* Guildford, UK: Department of Sociology, University of Surrey.

Goldner, S. (2007). Mixed method research. *Journal of Health Service Resource Policy, 12*(80), 168.

Groth, C., & Koch, K. (2010). When economic growth is less than exponential. *Economic Theory, 44,* 213-242.

Gruescu, S. (2007). Population aging and economic growth: Education policy and family policy in a model of endogenous growth. *Regional Science, 83*(4). 659-661.

Hagan, F. E. (2000). *Research methods in criminal justice and criminology.* Boston, MA: Allyn & Bacon.

Hammersley, M. (1996).The relationship between qualitative and quantitative research: Paradigm loyalty versus methodological eclecticism. In J. T. E. Richardson (Ed.), *Handbook of qualitative research method for psychology and social sciences* (pp. 159-174). Leicester, UK: British Psychological Society.

Hammersley, M., & Atkinson, P. (2005). *Ethnography: Principles in practice* (2nd ed.) New York, NY: Routledge.

Henderson, J., & Akers, M. (2009). Coming home to rural America: Demographic shifts in the Tenth District. *Economic Review-Federal Reserve Bank of Kansas City, 94*(3), 99-124.

Kinghorn, M., & Justis, R. (2008). How our population grows. *Indiana Business Review, 83*(2), 1-6.

Konstantinos, A. G. (2006). Tax-spending policies and economic growth: Theoretical predictions and evidence from the OECD. *European Journal of Political Economy, 23*(4), 885-902.

Landes, D. (2006). *The wealth and poverty of nations.* New York: W.W. Norton.

Lee, M. A., Harvey, M., & Neustrom, R. (2002). Local labor markets and caseload decline in Louisiana in the 1990s. *Rural Sociology, 67*(1), 556-577.

Lee, M. A., & Qusey, G. C. (2007). Size matters: Examining the link between small manufacturing, socioeconomic deprivation, and crime rates in nonmetropolitan communities. *Sociological Quarterly, 42,* 581-602.

Lee, R., & Mason, A. (2010). Fertility, human capital, and economic growth over the demographic transition. *European Journal of Population, 26,* 159-182.

Lincoln, Y.S., & Guba, E.G. (1985). *Naturalistic inquiry*. Beverly Hills, CA: Sage.

Lobao, L., & Hooks, G. (2003). Public employment, welfare transfers, and economic well-being across local populations: Does a lean and mean government benefit the masses? *Social Forces, 82*, 519-556.

Lucas, R. E. (1988). On the mechanics of economic development. *Journal of Monetary Economics, 22*(1), 3-42.

Lyson, T. A., & Tolbert, C. M. (2003). Small manufacturing and nonmetropolitan socioeconomic well-being. *Environment and Planning, 28*, 1779-1794.

Maestas, N., & Zissimopoulos, J. (2010). How longer work lives ease the crunch of population aging. *Journal of Economics Perspectives, 24*(1), 139-160.

Malthus, T. (1979). *An essay on the principal of population*. (P. Appleman, Ed.). Cambridge: Cambridge University Publishing.

Marder, M., & Bansal, D. (2009). Life and death during the Great Depression. *National Academy of Sciences of the United States of America, 106*(41), 17-90.

Marshall, G., & Rossman, G.B. (2006). Designing qualitative research, (4th ed.) Thousand Oak, Sage, CA.

Mencken, F. C. (2006). Federal spending and economic growth in Appalachian counties. *Rural Sociology, 65*, 126-148.

Mencken, F. C., Bader, C., & Polson, E. C. (2006). Integrating civil society and economic growth in Appalachia. *Growth and Change, 37*(1), 107-127.

Mitchell, W., & Mosler, W. (2006). Understanding the economic fallacies of the intergenerational debate. *Australian Journal of Social Issues, 41*(2), 160-170.

Mollick, A. V. (2006). The growth of Texas counties in the 1990s: The roles of county size and industry clusters. *The Review of Regional Studies, 36*(1), 87-120.

Paulson, M. B., & Toutkoushian, R. K. (2006). Economics and institutional research: Expanding the connections and applications. *InterScience*, 95-103.

Peat, J., Mellis, C., Williams, K., & Xuan W. (2002). *Health science research: A handbook of quantitative methods*. London, UK: Sage.

Peretto, P., & Seater, J. (2008). Factor eliminating technological change. Economic Research Initiative at Duke (ERID). Working Papers, No.1.

Pope, C., & Mays, N. (2005). Reaching the parts other methods cannot reach: An introduction to qualitative methods in health and health services research. *British Medical Journal, 32*(11), 42-45.

Prettner, K., & Prskawetz, A. (2010). Decreasing fertility, economic growth and the intergenerational wage gap. *Empirica, 37,* 197-214.

Rappaport, J. (2004). Why are population flows so persistent? *Journal of Urban Economic Growth, 56,* 554-580.

Sertich, J. (2004). New governance for a rural economy: Reinventing public and private institutions. Conference, May 17-18, 2004, Kansas City, Missouri.

Singleton, R. A., Jr., & Straits, B. C. (2005). *Approaches to social research* (4th ed.). New York: Oxford University Press.

Smith, A. (1976) *An inquiry into the nature and causes of the wealth of nations.* (J. C. Bullock, Ed.). New York, NY: P. F Collier & Son.

Tonnessen, M. (2008). The statistician's guide to utopia: The future of growth. *TRAMES, 2,* 115-126.

White, H., & Anderson, E. (2007). Growth versus distribution: Does the pattern of growth matter? *Development Policy Review, 19*(3), 267-289.

Woodward, D., Figueiredo, O. & Guimaraes, P. (2006). Beyond the Silicon Valley: University R & D and high-technology location. *Journal of Urban Economics, 60*(1), 15-32.

Yakita, A. (2006). Life expectancy, money, and growth. *Journal of Population Economics, 19,* 579-592.

Yin, R. K. (2003). *Research design and methods.* Thousand Oaks, CA: Sage.

Zhang, J., & Zhang, J. (2004). How does social security affect economic growth? Evidence from cross-country data. *Journal of Population Economics, 17,* 473-500.

Zhuang, H., & St. Juliana, R. (2010). Determinants of economic growth: Evidence from American counties. *The International Business and Economics Research Journal, 9,* 5.

APPENDIX A

Population and Economic Growth Survey

1. Are you male or female?
2. Are you in the farming or non-farming business or neither?
3. Are you between the ages of

    18-24 years
    25-34 years
    35-49 years
    50-64 years
    65 years and above

4. What types of tax data are used to define Pierce County's economic growth?

    Sales tax
    Property tax
    All of the above
    Not sure

5. Is the population of Pierce County declining?

    Yes
    No
    Not sure

6. If you indicated "Yes", please explain briefly.
   _____
   _____
   _____
   _____

7. Do you think the elderly population (68 years and older) in Pierce County, based on their retired income, will have adequate standard of living after retirement?

   Yes
   No
   Not sure

8. If you indicated either "Yes" or "No," briefly explain your answer.
9. On a scale of 1 to 10, 10 being the highest score, please rate the economic growth of Pierce County.

   1 2 3 4 5 6 7 8 9 10

10. Describe the mortality rate in Pierce County.

    Decreasing
    Increasing
    Not sure

11. Describe the fertility rate in Pierce County.

    Decreasing
    Increasing
    Not sure

12. On the issue of continued economic growth and controlled emigration in Pierce County, is a possible higher education institution, at least a two-year college, a desirable concept in Pierce County in the near future?

Yes
No
Not sure

13. Please list some ideas to help policymakers maintain economic growth in Pierce County and reduce the "brain drain" of skilled labor emigrating from Pierce County.

PROFILE

Name in Full:	Sunday Christopher Enubuzor, Ph.D.
Post Desired	Professor
Place of Birth	Lagos, Nigeria
Nationality	Nigeria/United States (Dual Citizen)
Marital Status	Married
Number of Age of Children	13, 14, 19, 25, and 29
Home and Postal Address	6421 Ranchview Lane, N; Maple Grove, MN 55311. USA
E-mail Address:	*senubuzor@yahoo.com*
Telephone Numbers	763-355-5513—Home; 763-868-6671—Cell

www.ingramcontent.com/pod-product-compliance
Lightning Source LLC
Chambersburg PA
CBHW030858180526
45163CB00004B/1629